BEHIND THE GREAT WALL

An Appraisal of Mao's China

LORENZ STUCKI

Behind the

AN APPRAISAL

Great Wall

OF MAO'S CHINA

TRANSLATED BY JEAN STEINBERG

FREDERICK A. PRAEGER, *Publishers*

New York · Washington

BOOKS THAT MATTER

Published in the United States of America in 1965
by Frederick A. Praeger, Inc., Publishers
111 Fourth Avenue, New York 3, N.Y.

Second printing, 1966

Library of Congress Catalog Card Number: 65-24935

This English-language edition is a revised, expanded version of
Land Hinter Mauern—China Heute, published by
Buchverlag der Neuen Zürcher Zeitung, Zürich, 1964.

This book is Number 168 in the series
Praeger Publications in Russian History and World Communism

Printed in the United States of America

Contents

1

The Fish and the Dragon

Estimates of Red China's population range from 600 to 700 million. One out of every four babies born today is Chinese. By far the largest nation in the world, the Chinese live on a territory of approximately 3.77 million sq. mi. Red China is the third-largest country after the Soviet Union (8.6 million sq. mi.) and Canada (3.85 million sq. mi.); it is larger than the United States and Great Britain combined. Its army, estimated at 2.7 million, is the biggest standing army in the world. In the fall of 1964, China became

1

an atomic power. Led by fanatically doctrinaire Communists, it has become the most aggressive of all nations, the breeding ground of many of the violent revolutionary upheavals that are disrupting the world today. Conflicts and disagreements between countries or governments are not unusual phenomena, but Red China is the only country whose leadership openly defends the proposition that war is a useful means of politics, suited, yes, even necessary to, the achievement of ideological objectives. The rulers of China do not have in mind a "big" war, which, lacking the technical equipment, they cannot wage, but rather revolutionary, civil-warlike guerrilla war. But this only makes their aggressiveness more uncanny, for this type of warfare spreads throughout a country like an invisible epidemic and cannot be fought by classical military tactics or modern superweapons.

Although we in the West are confronted by it daily, we know very little of present-day China. It is a blank page in the book of our general knowledge, a mysterious something, behind whose now smiling, now threatening exterior we imagine all kinds of evil. The dragon, the traditional symbol of China, has taken on a profound meaning. The unknown, coming uncomfortably close, makes us fearful. It becomes an eerie, irrational nightmare.

What kind of animal is this dragon?

A Backward Look at Recent History

In the nineteenth century, when the Western powers fanned out into all corners of the globe in search of power and wealth, China had a two-thousand-year-old cultural tradition. The Chinese had invented gun powder and rockets. Their contributions to philosophy, science, and art were impressive, but militarily and industrially they lagged behind the West. Throughout its history, China had looked upon itself as the "Middle Kingdom," bordered by vassal states and barbarian peoples. No power comparable in either size or rank was close to it. Measured against Chinese culture, the only valid yardstick, the white people from the far-away West were also inferior barbarians. However, these barbarians soon proved to be superior militarily. They extracted one concession after another; they assumed special economic rights and, ultimately, territorial privileges. The center of China's largest city and port, Shanghai, for example, became "extraterritorial," i.e., a walled-in foreign territory under foreign administration, ruled over by foreign police and troops. A proud, self-confident, highly civilized people was humiliated in a manner unprecedented in the annals of history.

At first China stood defenseless, but later it began to look into the reasons for Western superiority and to learn from the foreigners, not because it wished to emulate the West, but in order one day to defeat it with its own weapons.

The empire proved incapable of asserting itself, and in 1911, it was overthrown in a revolution led by Sun Yat-sen, the founder of the Kuomintang, whose goal was the renewal of China and its inner strengthening against the foreign invaders. The immediate aftermath of the overthrow of the monarchy was merely the abolition of centralized rule, which had served to preserve the unity of the country. The revolution did not mean unequivocal victory of the forces intent upon modernization. The Kuomintang government set up headquarters in Canton, and until 1928, an opposition government ruled in Peking. During this period, ambitious politicians and war lords in various provinces of this huge country declared themselves independent and ruled independently. The vitality of the nation exhausted itself in internal power struggles. It took two decades before the Kuomintang government, under Chiang Kai-shek, Sun Yat-sen's successor, was able to gain control over all of China. But in the meantime, a new enemy and rival force had come into being: the Communist Party, organized in the early 1920's, in the wake of the Russian revolution. Sun Yat-sen had formed an alliance with the Soviet Union against the common enemy, the West. But after his death (1925), the Kuomintang more and more sought the support of the Chinese national bourgeoisie and business community in its battle against the military and the feudal lords. Without the backing of this bourgeoisie, political and economic rebirth seemed impossible. But these were the very groups that opposed a radical left course. There followed a break with the Communists, and attempted Communist rebellions in a number of the larger cities were put down ruthlessly by Chiang Kai-shek.

China was primarily an agricultural country with little industry, and as long as the Communist Party followed the orthodox Marxist pattern of recruiting its members solely from among the urban proletariat it remained weak. But one of its lesser leaders, Mao Tse-tung, decided to win the peasants over to the cause of Communist revolution, *against* the wishes of the Party's Central Committee and *against* the dictates of Moscow. In the two decades of internal disorder and civil war, the misery of rural China had increased. Countless peasants were hopelessly indebted to money lenders, big landowners, and corrupt local officials. Mao Tse-tung's program—land for the landless, the canceling of debts, and the expulsion of local bureaucrats—was a message the peasants understood, even though they were illiterate and unable to follow abstract Marxist theory.

Partisan Warfare

The Communists recruited their first armed soldiers in the vast open, inaccessible rural areas. Gaining temporary control of individual villages, they implemented the promised reforms. News of this spread like wildfire by word-of-mouth in the surrounding countryside—a highly developed technique in countries without local newspapers. Highly disciplined Party cadres saw to it, by force if necessary, that none of their people profited personally. The "Red" soldiers did not loot. They even introduced a new and unheard-of practice: although armed, they paid for what they ate or took from shops. As a matter of fact, they even paid for or repaired damages. This was more persuasive than all propagandistic promises. The people, accustomed to a looting, unscrupulous soldiery, became convinced that the Communists (the peasants knew very little else about them) were for them, that they were different and better than anyone else before them, that they represented the hope for a better future.

In the long run, this discipline enforced by Mao and his followers probably was instrumental in turning the tide of the Civil War. The partisans, so said Mao, are the fish, and the population is the water in which they swim. If the temperature of the water is conducive, the fish thrive and multiply. Communist strategy, which from the very outset was not so much military as political-psychological, sought to create a hospitable water temperature, so that the active Communist partisans, although a small minority, could gain popular support. This tactical lesson of psychological-political revolutionary warfare still is of central importance in the methods of the Chinese Communists (in contrast to the Russian Communists) and in their approach to the problem of achieving power through "military class struggle." It is being applied in South Vietnam and eventually might be applied in the rest of southern Asia, Latin America, and Africa.

When Chiang Kai-shek realized the significance of the Communist peasant organizations, the "Red" guerrillas had already become strong in a number of provinces, particularly in Kiangsi in southeastern China. They controlled large rural areas and had won the sympathy and support of the local population, which kept them informed and hid them when they were in trouble. Chiang Kai-shek launched a number of large-scale military operations against the Communist-held territories, but without any real success. The guerrillas, shunning open combat, ambushed small government troop units and attacked supply trains, thus acquiring much-needed arms. By 1934, six different "soviets," Communist-governed miniature states with a total population of 9 million, were set up, Mao Tse-tung was "head" of a Communist "government" in Kiangsi Province that ruled over large parts of the area.

Now Chiang Kai-shek changed his strategy, adapting it to guerrilla tactics. At the same time, the Communists, following the advice of their dogmatic leaders and of Moscow, and against the wishes of Mao Tse-tung, engaged in some major battles and suffered defeat at the hands of the government troops. Kiangsi, the seat of Communist power, was surrounded and squeezed. The end seemed only a matter of time.

Desperate, the Communists decided to attempt a breakthrough and fight their way to the west toward more inaccessible terrain, where attacks against them could not be launched so easily. On October 16, 1934, the 90,000-man Chinese Red Army began its famous Long March via eastern Tibet to north Shensi, a distance of nearly 6,000 mi., crossing high mountains and raging rivers, swamps and arid steppes, constantly fighting the pursuing government troops and hostile local detachments. At the end, 7,000 men were left. But in the course of this trek, Mao Tse-tung became the unchallenged leader of the Chinese CP; his theory on guerrilla warfare and the mobilization of the peasants triumphed over the old, Western Soviet ideas of the revolution of the urban proletariat and became one of the dogmas of Chinese Communism.

Fight Against Japan

Meanwhile, in 1931, Japan, coming from Korea, occupied Manchuria, the most industrialized region of China. On March 1, 1932, Japan proclaimed Manchuria an independent state under Japanese control and renamed it Manchukuo. Chiang Kai-shek's government, fighting for the unity of the country against war lords and against the Communists, was too weak to resist the militarily and technically superior Japanese, and the West deserted China. The League of Nations issued empty protests. But despite this new humiliation, the reform and modernization of China continued to progress, albeit slowly. The government even succeeded in acquiring some Western capital for industrialization. But history did not grant Chiang Kai-shek, who strove for the national renewal and strengthening of China under the banner of anti-Communism and anti-imperialism, much time.

A year after the end of the Long March, Germany and Japan concluded the anti-Comintern pact, an alliance against the Soviet Union and international Communism, and in line with the old saying "The enemies of my enemies are my friends," the fronts in the Far East also re-formed. In the face of the danger posed by Japan, China and the Soviet Union entered into an alliance, and on orders of Stalin, the Chinese Communists made a truce with Chiang Kai-shek. Simultaneously, some of the European sources of capital, more sympathetic to the "anti-Communist" Hitler than to "Stalin's friend" China, withdrew their economic support.

Eight months after the conclusion of the German-Japanese pact, on July 26, 1937, Japanese troops moved on Peking. For eight years, in the course of which large parts of the country were occupied, China fought a life-and-death battle against Japan, a battle in which China stood alone until Pearl Harbor. The Communists, more experienced in guerrilla warfare than the government troops, helped in the fight against the Japanese, but they never forgot to make propaganda capital out of their help, their "patriotism," their antifascist convictions, their plans for a better, modern, strong China, and they did not fail to broaden their base.

Mao's Victory

On August 6, 1945, the first atom bomb ever dropped destroyed the Japanese city of Hiroshima. On August 8, the Soviet Union declared war against Japan and entered Japanese-occupied Manchuria. On September 2, the Japanese plenipotentiary signed Japan's unconditional surrender.

Chiang Kai-shek's China was one of the victorious powers. But after eight years of war, the country was exhausted and faced with insoluble problems. This was the chance the Communists looked for.

The Communist armies, which even while fighting Japan had never subordinated themselves to the government troops, now were given the Japanese arms captured by the Soviet Union in Manchuria; thanks to the Soviet occupation, they controlled large areas of Manchuria and much of the countryside in the rest of China, except for the big cities. They used the same tactics which had served them so well in the early 1930's in Kwangsi. The Kuomintang government, militarily depleted by the war, could not assert itself against them. It lost authority among a population yearning for peace and order. President Truman sent General Marshall to China in an attempt to mediate between Chiang Kai-shek and Mao Tse-tung. Although the United States extended economic and arms aid to the Kuomintang government, its wartime ally, it did not pit its power against the Communists. The United States was still trying desperately to preserve its wartime alliance with the Soviet Union in the name of peace and international order and within the framework of the United Nations. Furthermore, at that time, so soon after the defeat of Hitler, public opinion in the West preferred the "antifascist" Communists to the right-wing, authoritarian, "reactionary" government of Chiang Kai-shek. Also, the Americans, who had just finished fighting an entirely different kind of war, did not understand the nature of a Communist guerrilla civil war, nor did they understand the real objectives of the Chinese Communists, those "land reformers" waging a more or less just social fight against an obsolete *ancien régime*.

Thus the Kuomintang government could never really consolidate and stabilize its forces. Its feeble strength was depleted by the fight against the Communists instead of being devoted to reconstruction and to urgent reforms, particularly on the land. Confidence in the Kuomintang, and of the Kuomintang in itself, waned; amid this defeatist climate, corruption grew. The Communists emerged as the symbol of the new future and impressed the people with their rigid discipline.

On January 22, 1949, Mao Tse-tung's troops entered Peking. On August 6—long after the American-Soviet honeymoon in Europe had come to an end as a result of the Communist coup in Czechoslovakia, the Berlin Blockade, and the air lift, and after the United States had formed NATO in defense against aggressive Communism—U.S. Secretary of State Dean Acheson announced that his country would no longer support the reactionary clique of Chiang Kai-shek. The victory of Communism probably could not have been staved off anyway, except, perhaps, with massive American support, but the American position made the cause of the Kuomintang seem a lost and hopeless one. At the end of the year, Chiang Kai-shek had to give up the mainland. He withdrew to the island of Formosa with the remnants of his army and a million refugees. China had become Communist. Mao's fish had conquered the dragon.

The New Imperialism

Since then, much water has flown along the banks of the Yangtze. The distributed land, with which the Communists had won over the peasants, was taken away from them in exchange for Party-controlled collective farms. The intellectuals and middle class, who fought for the "reformers" and "liberators" from feudal backwardness and family tyranny, were muzzled and re-educated, and many who, encouraged by Mao, criticized the regime in 1957, were arrested. The transition from Socialism to true Communism, launched in 1958–59 with people's communes and the "Great Leap Forward," was temporarily shelved when it proved impracticable, but there was none of the ideological loosening up and relative "liberalization" which changed the face of the Soviet Union and Eastern Europe after Stalin's death. On the contrary, after 1960, the conflict between the Soviet Union, whose leaders were preaching "peaceful coexistence" with capitalism, and Red China, which stood for violence and revolutionary war, intensified, and the

Middle Kingdom isolated itself from the capitalist-democratic world as well as from most of its Communist allies. Does present-day China think that it can successfully defy the rest of the world?

China has not forgotten the humiliation inflicted on it by the world—by the West, Japan, Czarist Russia, and Communist Russia. After 1911, it struggled in vain through nationalist renewal, domestic reforms, and large-scale modernization to become strong enough to make its mark in the world, to become respected and not have to suffer the insults of foreign "barbarians." Without question, Mao Tse-tung has succeeded in this. After almost forty years of civil strife and wars, China once more is a unified country under strong and disciplined leadership; it has driven out the arrogant foreigners (along with those eager to help), and it is respected, even feared, by the rest of the world. In the old days, there were foreign clubs, for example in Shanghai, which had signs on their doors saying "Dogs and Chinese not allowed." Today, large areas of China are barred to foreigners, and admission to others is granted only fitfully and by special permission. China's self-confidence and pride have been restored, although at a very high price indeed, and after many years of being the victims of arrogance the new rulers have themselves become arrogant, both in their roles as Chinese and Communists.

Being confirmed Marxists, they believe that the world, following predetermined laws of history, will one day become Communist, and that they are pre-destined to become the supreme rulers in that future world because:

1. China, the Middle Empire, the most populous nation with an ancient civilization, is entitled to first place in that world.

2. The Soviet Russian Communists, having become increasingly bourgeois, material, and coexistence-oriented, have betrayed the central principles of Marxism, the Chinese leaders are the sole trustees of the true and absolute teachings, the only conscious and active propagators of the law according to which world history develops.

3. Mao Tse-tung has supplemented Marx's teachings through his development of guerrilla-warfare methods, the only methods suited to countries without a powerful industrial working class, and the success of the "fish."

But what is the reality, the power, the economic potential and domestic strength behind this missionary imperialism? What is present-day China, the mysterious, obscure dragon, really like?

2

Underdevelopment

Red China is barred to the outsider not merely by the "Bamboo Curtain," an innocuous enough designation for a wall even more solid than the Iron Curtain. It is barred by many walls. Once the visitor has obtained his visa and crosses the border, his problems really begin. A visa is not a magic key that opens up the door to the country. It is merely a document entitling the visitor to go to a specified city or cities—in my case Canton, which is on the way from Hong Kong, and Peking, China's capital. If one wishes to go anywhere else but the places specified, special permission, which may be granted for some cities but not for others, must be obtained. And in order to obtain this special permission, one must have additional special travel documents.

Even more forbidding than the walls within walls is the official Chinese travel agency, which, in all fairness, does take care of such essentials as interpreters, hotel accommodations, and railway and theater tickets, quite efficiently. But the foreign visitor is made utterly dependent on it; he cannot escape its ministrations, and soon he realizes that the attention lavished on him is a device meant to isolate him from everyday China. The interpreter waiting for the visitor on the station platform or at the airport may be good or bad, pleasant or disagreeable, but always impersonal. He has obviously been forbidden to have any personal contact with his charge. He will not let you treat him to a glass of beer; you cannot have a frank conversation with him; it is impossible to find out what he really thinks and believes. Moreover, these official guides are also busily engaged in erecting walls around their clients. Should you be so bold as to express a desire to eat in a restaurant frequented by local people instead of at the hotel, he will try to dissuade you. If he fails in this, he will see to it that, once at the restaurant, you are seated in a separate room. At the theater, during intermissions, he will take you to a special room, away from the curious stares of the audience, and cater to you as if you were a V.I.P. At a performance in a Nanking theater attended by several Western visitors and a group from Guinea, two such private rooms were made available: one for the whites, the other for the Africans. Railroad stations, too, have private waiting rooms, and on arrival or departure, foreign visitors are taken past the queue of ordinary travelers through a separate entrance or exit. On trains, a foreigner wishing to have his meals served in the dining car instead of in his very own private compartment must be extremely persistent.

Propaganda

The hardest wall to break through is the propaganda barrier. Whether visiting a nursery school or a university, a factory, hospital, or people's commune, the routine invariably is the same; the visitor is shown to a reception room where the chief administrator or his deputy, in the presence of at least two other men or women, delivers a standard talk, to wit: "Before Liberation," none of this existed; there was only a dilapidated workshop, and everybody was exploited by the imperialists and their lackeys, etc.; but "after Liberation," everything was expanded and improved. "Liberation," of course, refers to the Communist takeover in 1949. As a rule, the factual content of this propaganda package is exceedingly skimpy. Whenever I tried to extract additional information by persistent questioning, I was treated to a fresh torrent of catch phrases or was refused a reply, either because I was not supposed to be told certain facts and figures or simply because my informant himself did not know the answer.

The Vacuum

The visits to schools, factories, hospitals, handicraft shops, etc., do not open up anything. On the contrary, by erecting glittering props, they isolate, they delimit the field of vision. It is impossible to find out or even sense what is in the minds of the people. But the pap handed out is so cliché-ridden, it is such an incredibly impersonal, Party-made, tape-recorded recital, that one cannot possibly believe that a real, living, flesh-and-blood human being is talking behind the façade. There is no personal contact, hardly even a glance, a smile, or a gesture. One experiences nothing, discovers nothing, learns nothing that is spontaneous, unrehearsed, natural, and open— except perhaps for the friendliness of the little three-year-old girl on the train from Canton to Peking, who stared at me in fascination, came toward me, held out her hands, and never took her eyes off me. But even during this episode, which anywhere else, despite all language barriers, would have evoked a spontaneous reaction on the part of the adults present—her parents, the dining-room waiters, and the other passengers—there was only rigid aloofness. Had I not met the warm and gay Chinese of Hong Kong, Formosa, and Southeast Asia and the Japanese, I might have come to believe that this aloofness was part of the East Asian nature. But that simply is not so. On the contrary: what we Westerners find so fascinating about East Asia—at least this side of the Bamboo Curtain—is the relaxed manner of the people, their ability to enjoy life, without anxiety and tension, whether in the extrovert vein of Bangkok or the reserve of the Japanese. Their spontaneity, genuineness, and sense of beauty endow even—or particularly—that which we think of as poverty and material backwardness with a captivating charm and inner joy. According to past visitors, all these qualities were also to be found in China, and especially in Peking. Today there is no trace of this. The people do not enjoy life. If they work, they do so joylessly, because they are not working for themselves and their families but under the pressure of "norm fulfillment." If they do not work, they are not leisurely, merely bored. One of the unenviable permanent Western correspondents in Peking, a man who knew pre-Communist China, told me: "They have killed hope." Life has lost all promise of future happiness and betterment. It has lost the sense of the unexpected and thus also the sense of excite-

A typical middle-class street in the old quarter of Peking.

A main thoroughfare in Peking.

ment and interest. There is no magic and no fascination. Life has become an abysmal bore.

The dullness of Chinese cities, including Peking and Shanghai, is underlined by the lack of all those things that lend sparkle to the appearance of other cities: pretty girls; elegant women; an occasional whiff of the perfume of the mysterious world outside; elegant shop windows; antique shops in which one can make a great find; bookstores in which one likes to browse because they are not stocked solely with monotonous, stereotyped Party literature; a hidden small restaurant; somebody singing in a backyard instead of the blaring loudspeakers on the streets.

Of course this sort of atmosphere in itself serves to convey some feeling of China. Yet the Chinese people must have some unique qualities, and the fact that these are so inaccessible, that one cannot even get an inkling of them, is enough to drive one to distraction.

One evening, in Suchow, in a hurry to go to the theater, I ordered shrimps (which are usually very good in China) at my hotel. I was served tiny prawns in their shells which I could not remove with the clumsy Chinese chopsticks. It was like a symbol of the task the visiting journalist faces in today's China: in practically no time to extract from the tough shells as much meat as possible with one's fingers.

Despite all these obstacles, after two months of intensive digging and watching I did know a little more about Red China than I did before my stay. Many of my impressions are strong and unambiguous, but much remains uncertain and conjectural, based on observations rather than on established and verifiable fact. I have often asked myself how well the Chinese themselves, including their Communist leaders, really do know their gigantic country and its vast population. For the Chinese are not a particularly spontaneous people. From time immemorial, they have been accustomed to reveal their true thoughts and feelings only to those closest to them. By its very nature, totalitarian rule fosters camouflage and distortion. Thus, the foreign visitor has to resign himself to the fact that he will take home with him subjective impressions and only a smattering of objective facts.

Among the strong and definite impressions I gained, this one stands out: China is far less developed than is generally believed in the West. In my thousands of miles of travel by rail, I saw a total of three tractors, and only one of these was working. The usual form of transport is a cycle-rickshaw or cart, drawn by a horse or donkey in Peking and by people (often women) farther south. Trucks are a rarity. In my two months there, I saw only one bulldozer. Even in relatively modern factories, through which visitors are guided with pride, an astonishing number of tasks are performed by hand. Housing on the whole is unspeakably primitive. The overwhelming majority of the people, both in city and country, live as they have always lived, crowded together in wooden shacks with their large families.

The shortage of skilled labor and key personnel is more serious. Fairly new factories look like fifty-year-old plants. The machinery is neglected; piled-up equipment is rotting away in filthy yards. Productivity is amazingly low and the general quality of goods very poor.

The Lack of an Elite

There are numerous reasons for this backward state, and not all of them are the fault of the regime. One must not forget that ever since the 1911 revolution, China was ravaged by civil war, and from 1937 to 1945, it fought the Japanese invaders, who occupied large areas of the country. Then came another four years of civil war. In the fifteen years of peace following these thirty-eight years of war, some progress has undoubtedly been made. But fifteen years is a very short time, particularly in a nation suffering from shortages of capital, trained labor, experienced managers, and technicians. The 1960 withdrawal of Russian technicians, most of whom took their plans with them, doubtless was a great setback. After 1960, much of the promised equipment and spare parts was not delivered; moreover, China had paid dearly for the development aid supplied by the Soviet Union in the preceding years.

Yet the system itself must bear much of the responsibility for China's backwardness. The intellectual, economic, and administrative elite that China once possessed was wiped out by the Communists: some were killed, others fled to Formosa or Hong Kong, and still others were simply pushed aside. Frequently their positions were filled by men appointed because of their political reliability or loyalty, or by Civil War army officers, or by men whose gifts were solely ideological. Among these were some, barely literate, who had acquired their elementary education in night courses. A director of a machine plant in Taiyuan, for example, could not tell me how many engineers were employed in his factory. He said that his (rather small) plant produced the steel needed for the production of the machines—I wondered whether in the canteen oven. A plant like this of course reflects its management: expensive machinery from the Soviet Union , Czechoslovakia, East and West Germany, Switzerland, and other countries stands in new workrooms, but only one in ten is in operation, and only one worker in ten is doing anything, while nine others stand around making conversation. Rusty metal parts, replacement parts, and semifinished products are heaped on the floor. But a state enterprise has no competitor and therefore cannot become bankrupt, and its director retains his post if his ideological fervor pleases his technically equally incompetent Party bosses.

Another reason for the general backwardness is the "Great Leap Forward," launched by Peking in 1958–59. This all-out effort to cut the Gordian knot of economic backwardness and to achieve in a brief span a level of economic development that normally would take three or four times as long plunged the country into a serious economic crisis. Stymied by a shortage of raw materials and equipment, construction on countless houses and factories was halted midstream. The country's economic structure was plunged into hopeless chaos. And because the peasants in the newly established people's communes offered passive resistance and because overzealous Party bureaucrats bungled agricultural planning, shifting manpower to the production of useless steel in blast furnaces instead of making it available for the planting of rice, the country found itself on the brink of famine.

Faced with catastrophe, the government reversed itself and stopped "leaping." Today, after a concentrated drive for agricultural and primary consumer-goods production, there is enough to eat and there are enough goods available to satisfy somewhat the modest purchasing power and quality standards of the people. But as a consequence of this shift, industrial expansion came to a virtual standstill. This may explain the astonishing number of people between the ages of twenty and forty loafing about in Chinese cities. But, of course, officially there is never any unemployment in a Communist country.

Another striking feature and yet another cause of the country's economic backwardness is the widespread laziness. Anyone who has seen the marvelously efficient, industrious, and enterprising Chinese of Hong Kong and Southeast Asia cannot help but be startled by the common sight of three or five workers standing around idly and watching another one work. I conducted a sort of private survey during my railroad trips, counting those working in fields we passed and those sitting around chatting, resting, or watching. The percentage of those working ranged from 45 to 48. It would be pointless to compile such statistics in urban areas, since only the work done in the many small stalls and workshops is visible; work done inside houses cannot be seen. But as far as I can judge, the level of industriousness in towns seems to be even lower than in the country. And the situation in factories is very much the same.

The explanation is simple—and it strikes at the heart of Communism: the absence of material incentives. This is borne out by two different examples. Besides the collectivized land he works, every peasant is given a tenth of a mu of land (approximately 80 sq. yd.) for his own personal use. He may sell the produce from this small plot and his privately owned livestock in the free market. The result is that city markets are glutted with eggs from privately bred hens and with privately grown vegetables, while rice, flour, and cotton grown by the collective continue to be rationed. Going into town from a people's commune toward evening, one can see peasant families, children and grandmothers included, hard at work on their little piece of private land. Another example is provided by the Peking rickshaw drivers. They, too, are collectivized, and until the summer of 1962 they were paid a fixed wage, whether or not they transported passengers. Naturally, there was never a rickshaw to be found on the streets of Peking. Then the system was changed, and the drivers were paid a lower basic wage plus a bonus based on actual work performance. Overnight, rickshaws, repaired and freshly painted, reappeared on the streets, and drivers competed for passengers.

If the government would offer similar incentives in other areas as well, it could not fail to stimulate the dormant efficiency of the people, and then China's situation would improve rapidly, without any Big Leaps and without the whiplash of the totalitarian state.

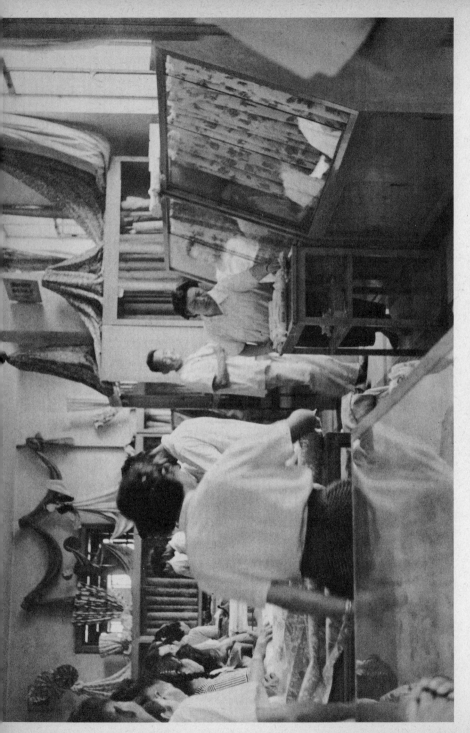

Rationed cotton yard goods in a department store.

3

After the Great Leap

Only once during my two months in China did I have
the chance to talk frankly with a more or less typical
ordinary Chinese. In the course of our conversation,
this twenty-five-year-old factory employee in southern
China, speaking English moderately well, grew more
daring and criticized some official policies. For that
very reason, I gave credence to what he said in defense of the government. Before the Communists took
over, he told me, his father, who had eleven children,
had a serious industrial accident that left him com-

pletely disabled; there was no social insurance and his employer paid him not a penny. Today, his father is taken care of by the government, which furnishes free medical care to the sick and disabled.

Wages and Prices

China's standard of living is still extremely low, even by Asian standards. In rural areas, where 90 per cent of the people live, it is considerably lower than in the cities. But compared to the indescribable misery, the total lack of rights or security of the very poor in the pre-Communist past, some progress has doubtless been made. The question remains, of course, whether totalitarianism has not been too high a price for this progress and whether more could not have been accomplished under a more open, less doctrinaire system.

The average wage of a skilled industrial worker is 60 yuan a month, or about $24. Except for apprentices, who earn only about 20 yuan, the lowest pay I heard of was 34 yuan, or about $14. Technicians get up to 120 yuan, and engineers up to 180 or even 250 yuan a month, depending on the type of factory. Interpreters working for the Chinese tourist agency are paid 60 to 80 yuan, a maid in a hotel for foreigners about 30. Top salaries of high-echelon government employees are nominally around 300 or 400 yuan, although their real income is probably double that because of the many special privileges, such as official cars.

What can this money buy? By Western standards, very little. If in the course of a single day you should decide to visit two factories and a nearby people's commune, the taxi fares alone will be equivalent to the average worker's monthly wage. A modest restaurant meal and a bottle of beer cost 3 to 5 yuan. Of course, the average Chinese never takes taxis, nor does he eat in "luxury" restaurants. How frugal his fare is can be judged from the fact that his canteen meals for an entire month cost 10 to 13 yuan—about as much as three to four meals at a restaurant. Rice, the Chinese food staple, is very cheap—0.15 yuan per lb. The cheapest meat costs about 1 yuan per lb. In looking at the price-wage structure, two factors must be borne in mind: both husband and wife usually are wage earners, but in addition to their numerous children, they frequently also support aged parents, aunts, and uncles.

Rice, flour, cotton, and a number of other goods in various localities are rationed. Obviously, these items must be in short supply, yet given these shortages, equal rationing is a socially just measure and as such represents progress. In the past, when there were poor harvests and famines, the prices simply climbed up, and the rich could buy whatever they wanted. Some became rich as the prices mounted. The mass of the people went hungry and some starved to death. Many measures we in the West take for granted and do not think of as "Communist" were introduced in China only after the Revolution.

Let us look at some consumer-goods prices: a pair of shoes costs 20 yuan; trousers, 40; a shirt, 20; a man's jacket, 40 to 60; a woman's coat, 120; a small transistor radio, 150; a tiny television set, 510; a yard of cotton, 1.30 to 1.50; a yard of silk, 3. These are average prices for average goods, though by Western standards their quality is poor.

Housing, heavily subsidized by the government, is very cheap. Factory managers told me that in factory-owned housing, workers pay only 2 to 3 yuan monthly per room: the area allotted for each adult is 3 to 4 sq. yd.; dormitories for unmarried workers cost only about 0.4 yuan per person, and three to six people share a single room.

A Worker's Budget

A foreigner can talk to and see the apartments of carefully screened and rehearsed workers only. Their homes are usually hung with innumerable pictures of Mao, work diplomas, and similar decorations, and their incomes are above average. Hence, what workers told me about their family budget in the presence of my official interpreter and two or three plant managers is at best typical only of the upper echelons of the working class. For example: Family X, which lives in the Shanghai area, consists of a man, his wife, a girl of eight, and a boy of three. The father earns 89 yuan a month in the factory; the mother does not work. They pay 7 yuan a month for their one-room flat, plus another 3 for water and electricity. They spend from 40 to 50 yuan on food, 1 yuan on soap and cleansers, 5 on cigarettes and sundries. The boy attends a free nursery school (the obviously upper-class nursery school in Peking which is shown to visitors charges a fee of 20 yuan a month). The only cost there is about 1 yuan for materials. The family spends from 10 to 20 yuan a year for clothing—the cost of a half a pair to one pair of shoes. The parents of both the man and his wife are also employed and therefore do not have to be supported. Thus, the X family should be able to put aside at least 20 yuan each month. Since Mr. X said that he saved only about 100 yuan annually, which he banks at 5 per cent interest toward the future purchase of furniture and a sewing machine, he probably was not quite candid about his expenditures. Of course, he is a Party member.

The cost-of-living picture becomes a little more cheerful when one remembers that elementary education is free, that workers get free hospital care, medicines, etc., and that their dependents get medical services at half price. Also, the government furnishes free or low-cost entertainment—all propaganda, of course.

On the other hand, a worker gets no vacation unless his dependents live in another town. In that case, he is allowed two weeks plus traveling time, with his fare paid by the factory. And even the proudly exhibited model dwellings, although unquestionably an improvement over the usual hovels, are primitive by Western standards. The tiny kitchens have no ovens, just small wood-burning stoves; the baths have only tiny washtubs, like those in laundry rooms, and even in cities like Shanghai, Wuhan, Sian, and Taiyuan, which have very cold winters, the new model housing developments are unheated.

A single observation offers a revealing commentary on the standard of living in China today: in hotels, restaurants, and dining cars, waiters, especially those who do not as a rule serve foreigners, simply cannot understand why "immensely rich" travelers fail to order ten-course dinners. The Chinese dream of wealth is much and good food.

Strangled Development

China, of course, is still a developing country, and it would be only logical if, like any other such country that is short of capital, it siphoned off a substantial portion of the national income for investment in urgently needed industrial development. The fact is, however, that industrial expansion came to a virtual stop after the economic catastrophe brought on by the Big Leap Forward. It is impossible to obtain any figures whatever about the funds channeled into national industrial investments. Western experts, diplomats, and foreign correspondents—Russians included—venture only vague estimates. The freeze on industrial development is official policy in Red China. As in everything else, there are slogans about it: "Adjustment-Consolidation-Filling the Gaps." A swing through the country shows that there are almost no new factories under construction and many lying idle or half-finished. Even in show plants through which visitors are taken, a great deal of the machinery is not in use. Plant production figures are simply unobtainable. At best, plant capacity is publicized. "Production is proceeding according to plan" is the usual formula, and questions about current production goals are brushed off with the explanation that figures have not yet been released. But it is obvious that the output in all capital-goods industries is very much below capacity. The one industrial sector that is really producing and expanding is that devoted to agricultural items, particularly chemical fertilizers, and probably the arms industry as well, particularly plants involved in the atomic-weapons program.

If those foreign experts who estimate that China's industry is working at no more than 50 per cent of capacity and that the annual investment rate is no more than 5 per cent of the national income are correct, then it becomes doubtful whether China can even keep pace industrially with its population increase, estimated at 10 to 12 million a year.

Admittedly, China offers a friendlier façade now that there is a breathing spell. There has been a letup since the hectic days of the Great Leap Forward. In the summer, more and more, splashes of color break the monotony of the dark blue attire worn by the majority, even though the women, with rare exceptions, continue to wear trousers, and pretty dresses or silk blouses are not to be seen anywhere. But the atmosphere now is a little less tense, and there are timid signs of a reawakening of the Chinese passion for gambling, strictly taboo until now. But will it last?

Another Leap?

Political motives make it improbable and—in view of China's great-power ambitions in South Asia, Africa, Latin America, and vis-à-vis the fraternal Soviet enemy—well nigh unthinkable that the Chinese economy can afford to mark time much longer. Should the government launch a new Leap Forward, perhaps in the next year or two, under another name, no doubt, and better prepared and with fewer errors of planning, the cost will have to be borne by the Chinese people, for there will be no Soviet aid this time. Should that happen, it would mean a lower standard of living either through a reduction in wages or an increase in the price of consumer goods. It is this prospect that makes the Chinese standard of living problematical. But how can it be forced down even more without bringing on new misery and, consequently, a step-up in the reign of terror?

China wants to become and must become an industrial country. But the closer it comes to this goal, the more critical the question of quality becomes—quality of labor, of materials, of machines, of maintenance, of management. Quality, however, cannot be achieved by Big Leaps Forward or by terror, but only through intrinsic, patiently nurtured growth.

Government officials talk of the "difficulties in construction" between 1960 and 1962, which, they say, were the result solely of natural catastrophes and the departure of Soviet technicians. This explanation may serve propaganda purposes, but there is the hint of a suspicion that the leadership itself seems to be at best half-convinced by this explanation. The people are told over and over again that all difficulties can be mastered by studying the writings of Mao Tse-tung and by the prerequisite Socialist enthusiasm, while foreign visitors are appalled by the incredible waste of time, energy, money, and materials, the handiwork of the many bureaucratic hacks well versed in ideological slogans but otherwise incompetent and unqualified. No country is less able to afford such waste than is China, with its enormous problems of development. And who picks up the tab for all these costly errors? The people, of course, just as they have done under the many inept dynasties throughout their long history.

(Top) The normal Chinese mode of moving things. (Bottom) A street in the heart of Peking.

Population Explosion and
Chemical Fertilizers

China is still a predominantly agricultural country and will probably remain so for another few decades. The failure of the Big Leap Forward demonstrated that the process of industrialization must be gradual, requiring continuous adjustments in the economy and the solution of extremely complex social, economic, and technical problems. Apparently the government has now come to understand this, but that does not necessarily mean that economic insights will never again be sacrificed to ideological considerations.

Since industrial progress at the present stage of development must perforce be very slow, large-scale mechanization of agriculture is neither feasible nor desirable. It is not feasible because China's industry cannot produce the 2–3 million items of farm machinery needed, because there is a shortage of fuel needed to run the machinery, and because it will take at least one or two generations for the hundreds of millions of Chinese peasants to acquire the technical skill to operate the machines. It is not desirable because industry could not absorb the agricultural labor force displaced by machinery in addition to the 10–12 million annual population increase. In fact there is very little machinery even in the model people's communes near the cities through which foreign visitors are shown. Harvesting is done with sickles, threshing with wooden boards, and plowing, at best, with oxen. The official spokesman who claimed that some 200 people's communes in the Shanghai area are 50 per cent mechanized was simply spreading one of the many crude, transparent lies being disseminated by the government. If it were true, there would be millions of unemployed.

Birth Control Propaganda

To all intents and purposes, "living standard" in China is merely another term for "nutrition level." Since even the privileged worker with an above-average income spends 60 per cent of his earnings on food, obviously a peasant with a monthly income of about $10 and with a minimum of two dependents (children or old people) will spend practically all his earnings on food. Thus, the average living standard depends on the ratio of population to agricultural production. This points up the two basic problems facing China —curbing the population explosion and increasing the yield of the land.

The government is actively encouraging birth control. Despite the prudery and puritanism of Communists everywhere, not just the Chinese, the subject is discussed quite openly in the newspapers and in organizations. Contraceptives are distributed for a pittance, women are urged to have themselves sterilized after the birth of their third child, and men are pressured into postponing marriage. An interpreter told me that the government did not want him to marry before the age of thirty-five. Until then, he was told, rather than father soldiers for his country—there are enough of those—he should devote his energies to learning languages and to perfecting his ideological chaperoning of foreign visitors.

In Shanghai, a not very ardent defender of the government (and hence a relatively reliable source) told me that the campaign had been a success locally. In some districts the birth rate had fallen to 1.2 per cent. Even in the country, most people were no longer having more than three or four children. If this is true, the problem may diminish in the future. But in the next fifteen or twenty years, today's children will be growing up and attempting to find a place for themselves in the economy. There are incredibly many of them. China is flooded with children. In the late afternoon and evening, after the schools, nurseries, and "children's palaces" have closed, every alley looks like a school yard during recess. And though it may be difficult to take a picture without getting a soldier in it (it is forbidden to photograph soldiers), it is utterly impossible during the later hours of the day to photograph a street scene without children in it. One has the impression that there are more children than grownups. And all of them must be fed, housed, educated, dressed, and given medical care. Family planning cannot have been in effect very long, if at all. Even the dark-blue pants worn by the women and girls (they must suppress their vanity as something bourgeois and decadent and conceal it behind a socialist façade) and the resulting difficulty in distinguishing between women and men do not seem to have helped to mitigate the population explosion.

Achievements of the Regime

Despite the Communists' glorification of the tractor, the motorized water pump has far greater significance for contemporary China. Rice, the main food staple,

requires intensive irrigation—as do corn, wheat, and
other grains grown in addition to rice in central China
and in place of rice in northern China—because of the
recurrent droughts in large areas of the country. Thus,
any increase in farm production largely depends on
water drawn from lakes or rivers or through drill
holes and pumped into large and small canals and
from these into the fields. Some of the pumps are
primitive devices powered by a man or woman on a
treadmill, but quite a few are motorized. An economic
official I interviewed put the aggregate horsepower
of pumps in China today at 6 million, a figure that
cannot of course be verified, and since he also claimed
that there were as many as 120,000 tractors in China
today, he was probably exaggerating. Still there can
be no doubt that much has been accomplished in this
area. Here the government has been much more sen-
sible and realistic than it would have us believe, since,
contrary to its own assertions, it has devoted more
energy to irrigation than to "tractorization."

Chemical fertilizers are another essential for increasing agricultural production. Of the many factories I saw, only two, chemical-fertilizer plants in
Shanghai and Sian, were beyond any doubt operating
at capacity. They are the only plants that were com-
pleted, and even enlarged, during the present halt in
industrialization.

Even after much poking around it is impossible to

find out how much chemical fertilizer is actually being produced. The official cited above gave an annual figure of more than 4 million tons. Assuming the total area under cultivation as 295 million acres, this means an average yearly use of 1 ton of fertilizer per 75 acres. But even this modest figure (in 1959, Taiwan used 1 ton of chemical fertilizer per 3.5 acres) does not seem to be accurate. According to the director of the Chinese-Albanian Friendship People's Commune, near Peking, doubtless a model commune, it uses 50 to 60 tons of chemical fertilizer a year for some 7,500 acres of cultivated land—an average of 1 ton for 125 to 150 acres. The national average is more likely to be half as much than twice as much. In 1959, China, according to figures compiled in Hong Kong, produced 700,000 tons of chemical fertilizer. Present output probably is somewhere between 1 and 2 million tons. But to achieve the rate of use reported for Taiwan in 1959, 80 million tons would be needed. Thus, the government's declaration that it can complete the process of "mechanization, irrigation, and chemical fertilization" of the farm economy within twenty to twenty-five years should be viewed with a certain degree of skepticism. But there can be no doubt that the government is attacking the problem of agricultural yield via chemical fertilizer production.

Afforestation

Finally, mention must be made of one campaign that, though perhaps of little propaganda value, may ultimately prove to be of considerable significance—afforestation. Apart from meeting industrial lumber demands, forests serve as a protection against wind and sand storms and erosion. The Ministry of Forests claims that some 295,000 acres of forests have recently been planted in western Manchuria, and 1.1 million in China's "Middle West" (Inner Mongolia, Shansi, Shensi, and Kansu). The trees planted are fast-growing species that require little water and thrive in sandy or loamy soil. "Forest walls" have been planted in some places (one of these, in northern Shansi, is 185 mi. long) to protect them against storms and the encroaching desert (stone walls have been erected for the same purpose); in others, small wooded tracts are created to protect individual villages and fields. Trees are being planted to hold down the soil along rivers and railroad beds, and city streets are being lined with trees. It seems that as a result of this program, the climate of Peking, a city plagued by dust because of the nearby desert, has already improved. However, there exist neither any comprehensive long-range plans nor any clear-cut ideas on the possible exploitation of climate control.

The Old and the New in the Villages

Unlike the cities, where new buildings—ugly and obsolescent though they may be—loom up here and there, the villages give the impression that almost nothing has changed in years or even centuries. There are the old huts of wood, clay, or stone, depending upon the local products (not to mention the many cave dwellings in Shensi province), the old village stores and teahouses, the superabundance of children and chickens, the small vegetable gardens, people carrying loads suspended from a pole balanced across their shoulders. The only new items are an occasional bicycle or radio, and here and there a cheap, mawkish color photograph of Mao Tse-tung.

But appearances are deceptive. Collectivization and the people's communes have wrought considerable changes in village life. Although the communes, after the initial fiasco, have become mere administrative bodies, and the village once more is the economic unit, it is nonetheless ruled by the Party and, moreover, is largely subordinate to the "production brigade," which comprises several villages ("teams"), and to the commune, which comprises several brigades. The creation of these two new bureaucratic echelons between village and district administration undoubtedly has helped to tighten the government's control over the countryside. Moreover, the goal of converting the commune into a giant state "factory" for the production of food has merely been postponed, not abandoned, since dogma decrees that in the Communist society of the future there will be no distinction between industry and agriculture, peasant and worker, town and country, and state ownership (or so-called people's ownership) is to replace collective ownership of land and the means of production.

Organization of the People's Communes

Needless to say, the selected communes shown to foreign visitors are not typical of the 70,000 Chinese communes, at least not so far as technical standards and productivity are concerned. Nevertheless, they do give some idea of how communes are organized. The Hoa Shan Commune near Wuhan on the Yangtze, to take an example, comprises 15 brigades and 138 teams. It has a population of 15,866 (3,813 families) and 2,500 acres under cultivation, mainly rice and wheat. Also, it has about 75 acres of orchards, and there is fishing in a few small lakes. The Ma Shi Sai Commune in the extremely fertile area of Sian has 19 brigades and 70 teams, 14,315 inhabitants (2,761 families), and almost 4,000 acres of corn, cotton, and vegetables. The 7,500 acres of cultivated land (grain, fodder, fruit, vegetables, livestock) in the Chinese-

A peasant selling vegetables from his private plot.

Albanian Friendship Commune near Peking are worked by only 5 brigades and 45 teams, made up of 24,000 people (5,400 families).

The team—as a rule, it is identical with the village —sells its produce to the state, pays the taxes, and distributes the net income to the members proportionate with the work contributed as it appears on the books. In the three above-mentioned communes, the peasants had an average annual income of 203, 400, and 322 yuan, respectively ($81.20, $160, and $128.80). This income must support two or three persons. Of course, it is supplemented by the private plots of about 80 sq. yd. per person, or 350 per family, on which vegetables and domestic animals, including pigs are raised. These plots, owned by the team but worked individually, account for 4 to 12 per cent of the entire team area, and the products grown on them may be consumed or sold on the open market.

Most teams cannot afford expensive equipment such as pumps and trucks; these are provided by the brigade or commune, which in turn gets its money partly from the team and partly from state subsidies. The land belongs to the team, but the machinery, schools, and hospitals, as well as certain special installations and workshops, are the property of the commune (or brigade), that is, the state. Some direct trade takes place between units. Thus, a team might sell its members' labor to other teams, charging them on an hourly basis, or a commune may sell an individual a young "state-owned" pig.

Where local Party bosses allow the village life to unfold and proceed cautiously with political indoctrination, the people's communes may eventually work out and even—from a purely economic point of view —be a success. Many urgent problems of development, such as the construction of large-scale irrigation systems operated by powerful pumps, obviously cannot be solved by individually operated farms; cooperative organization and a certain amount of state aid are essential. Indeed, since the government's recent tactical retreat, which restored to the village its traditional function and to the peasant a small plot of land for his private use, actual conditions in China may not differ too markedly from the mixed-economy systems based on private cooperatives found in a number of non-Communist developing countries. And therefore China now has enough food. But—and this is an important "but"—the administrative authority vested in the commune and ideological dogma give every inept and fanatical Party bureaucrat the power to inflict lasting harm on the farm economy, to stultify the cooperation of the population where that has slowly been built up, and to jeopardize all chances of success. The peasants have not forgotten that during the Civil War, the Communists won them over with the promise that the land would be theirs. The government's ultimate objective, taking away the small measure of self-determination still enjoyed by the village and the tiny plots of land, hangs over the heads of the peasants like the sword of Damocles.

5

From Kindergarten to University

Formal education in Communist China has two major goals: to build up the broadly based, highly qualified elite able to guide the nation's economic, technical, administrative, and political development, and at the same time to prevent the emergence of an elite likely to turn into a Soviet-style "new class," the breeding ground for the heresy of revisionism. The Chinese, insofar as they can at all see the inherent contradiction in these two aims, hope and believe that their ideology will help them surmount it. Others, Russians and East Europeans included, do not share their conviction.

Three- to seven-year-olds in China are as engaging as young children anywhere else; they are the only ones whose spontaneity has not yet been stifled, or at least dulled, by ideological pressures. After that (and in the case of boys sooner than girls), they become the victims of all the fears and inhibitions systematically drummed into the people: the foreigner he meets may be a spy or a class enemy; friendliness or spontaneous warmth might be compromising; any unauthorized or unsupervised venture into unfamiliar terrain may lead into a trap without your realizing how or why. Only very young children have not yet learned fear. But the efforts to inculcate it begin early. Ideological training starts in kindergarten. Pictures of Mao Tse-tung decorate the walls. The younger children (the three-year-olds) have a quarter-hour of political pre-indoctrination daily, and the older ones (up to six or seven years) a half-hour. They are taught to love Comrade Mao and the other leaders and their Communist fatherland, and certain associations are fixed in their young minds: the "Party" and "for the people" are equivalent to "good," and "class enemy," "exploiter," "imperialist," and "American" are "bad."

Political indoctrination proper begins in the primary schools. Moreover, all teachers, whatever their

Calisthenics in a primary school.

A kindergarten for children of the "new class" in Peking (above and on following page).

subject, are exhorted to contribute to the development of "Socialist consciousness." Woe to the teacher who does not fulfill his ideological norm. At the age of nine, most boys and girls—85 per cent, I was told— join the Young Pioneers. Of course the youngster who does not belong and cannot wear the lovely red tie feels like a pariah.

Through the Eyes of Children

Since foreign guests, especially the many delegations from Africa, Latin America, and South Asia, are always shown the same model schools, these visits invariably follow the same deadly routine. The principal, flanked by one or two persons whose functions are not too clearly defined, takes the visitor to a reception room with the inevitable portraits of Mao, Marx and Engels, Lenin and Stalin, and mechanically reels off a welcoming speech. On entering the classroom, the visitor is greeted by a well-drilled chorus of welcome followed by applause; on leaving, the scene is repeated.

One learns a bit more by asking to talk to individual students. The school official, though not prepared for such a request, does not dare to refuse it. I once tried to find out what two thirteen-year-old boys, picked by the teacher on my request, knew about the world. It was little enough. All they knew about Switzerland was that it was somewhere in Europe. They did not think much of France; their opinion of de Gaulle was a bit better. India was very bad, because it had pro- voked China, was rather capitalistic, and accepted U. S. dollars. Japan? Nothing. The Soviet Union? Though still a semi-socialist country, it was very badly governed. The archvillain, of course, was the United States, although they could not say just why.

In Shanghai, in a "children's palace," i.e., a rec- reation center for children, I was met by the director and two twelve-year-old girls who took my hands and told me that they had friends in all countries and wanted friendship with all nations. Even with the United States? Yes, they were for the American people but against their oppressors. How come, I asked them, that the American people elected oppressors to govern them? But here their Party-instilled knowledge was of no help, and the director quickly came to their rescue with the assertion that U. S. elections were not genu- ine.

My conversation with two students of a Peking sec- ondary school—a girl of seventeen and a youth of eighteen—was more fruitful. The director, knowing from sad previous experience of my insidious inter- rogations, had selected these two from among his 1,616 students. Switzerland, they knew, was moun- tainous, neutral, peace-loving, friendly toward China, and manufactured high-quality machinery; however, it was a capitalist country. Whether its Communist

Party was strong or weak they could not tell me, but they did know that a pro-Chinese Communist group had been formed. France was an imperialist power, but de Gaulle was a good man because he stood up to the United States. The American people were either very rich or very poor. Yugoslavia, under its traitorous leadership, was in the vanguard of those countries that were traveling the road from socialism to capitalism and, so they said, responsible for Soviet revisionism.

The director, of course, was present at all these interviews, which automatically ruled out any possibility of nonconformist answers. Nevertheless, a girl student of French at the University of Peking told me that before judging a country, one should get to know it well from personal experience—an excellent piece of advice, but one which Communist propaganda unfortunately will not heed.

The Educational System

In some of its aspects, China's school system resembles that of many Western countries. Children between the ages of three and six attend nurseries and kindergartens; from seven to twelve, primary school (divided into four-grade lower sections and two-grade upper sections; the two-year sections, however, do not exist everywhere, especially not in rural areas); then secondary school, comprising two three-year segments (intermediate and high); and finally university, for four, five, or six years, depending on the area of study. Generally, specialization begins only after the intermediate level, although there are specialized intermediate schools consisting only of the higher classes, i.e., after the age of fifteen. The official I interviewed at the Ministry of Education in Peking said that before the Communist "liberation," only 20 per cent of all children attended school, whereas now all can do so. Apparently at least four years of schooling is compulsory, although despite repeated questioning I could not get either a confirmation or denial, perhaps because there are still far too few schools and teachers, or perhaps because government officials, unable to understand the way we think, shy away from the word "compulsory" lest we take it as proof of their totalitarianism.

Besides the regular schools, where every subject is steeped in ideology, adult education is being promoted through evening schools. Moreover, in Peking and some other cities, a "Television University" has for some time been offering extension courses of one-and-a-half to two hours daily for persons with an intermediate education, even enabling them to take university examinations. A senior television official in Peking asserted that more than 10,000 people are already taking these courses, and the Ministry of Education claims that hundreds of thousands of people are taking evening university courses. (More precise figures are unobtainable.)

The figures are invariably impressive. Since 1949, it is claimed, more than 100 million illiterates have been taught to read and write, and attendance at universities has increased sixfold, at intermediate schools fivefold, and at primary schools threefold. (If the rate of primary school attendance in 1949 was only 20 per cent, this would put the present figure at 60 per cent and not 100.) The quality of instruction still seems fairly low, no doubt in part because of the dearth of qualified, politically untainted teachers, and in part because of the disproportionate amount of time and energy devoted to ideological drivel. Some of the interpreters assigned to escort me and other journalists, fully trained linguists though they were, spoke French or English no better than graduates of European high-schools. In Taiyuan, not having a professional interpreter, I was accompanied by an instructor in English at the university whose linguistic facility would barely qualify him for a job as a Swiss hotel clerk.

The scarcity of good teachers is in part a direct result of the political climate. The educated elite of pre-Communist China—i.e., those still in the country—is viewed with suspicion. Because its members compromised themselves either in the early days of the regime or during the short-lived "Hundred Flowers" campaign, they are regarded as unworthy of molding the future "standard bearers of the revolution." Before 1949, many of the best schools in China were mission schools (21 universities, 514 intermediate and high schools, and 1,133 primary schools), some of them under foreign auspices. Their 380,000 students, according to an education official, were brought up in "awe of foreign imperialists and aggression against China," and some were actually trained as "agents." Some of the former teachers have been— and still are being—"retrained," but they probably are not the most able, intelligent, and best. Instead, deserving fighters from the ranks of workers and peasants have been turned into teachers in "big leaps forward."

The Fear of a New Elite

In China, scholars have traditionally stood high in the social scale, if only because the mastery of several thousand written characters is in itself a formidable achievement. For their part, they felt only contempt for the common man engaged in manual labor. This strong tradition has created a serious problem for the government. Until recently, 80 per cent of those admitted to high schools and universities had to have a working-class or peasant background. The result was that hundreds of thousands of young Chinese suddenly found themselves on a higher social level than their parents. It is a truism that no one is as acutely class-conscious as the person who has risen above the station into which he was born, and the fact is that these young people have tended toward arrogance, class feelings, and disdain for the proletariat—an utterly intolerable situation for a government calling itself a dictatorship of the proletariat.

The problem does not readily lend itself to a sociological solution. The 80 per cent provision was dropped recently because of the poor student material. But selection based on merit also had undesirable consequences: suddenly the high schools and universities were overrun by the sons and daughters of the former bourgeoisie, who proved even less reliable in obeying the Party line, considered themselves an elite group, and, like the "revisionist" young people in the Soviet Union, showed greater interest in jazz than in dialectical materialism and the writings of Mao Tse-tung. Since the beginning of 1964, the students from the proletariat are once again being given preference.

The regime's main weapon against the emergence of a social elite is compulsory "productive labor." High-school students and Party officials must spend one month, and university students from one to one-and-a-half months each year at manual labor in factories or people's communes. The students obviously do not like it and lose valuable time in the process. In questioning managers of factories and communes, I gathered that these reluctant and inexperienced "volunteers" were a hindrance rather than a help. However, the government hopes to prevent this badly needed elite of specialists and technicians from becoming a new class. The ideological aim is the creation of proletarian intellectuals and intellectual proletarians. The alarm over the emergence of a new bourgeoisie in Yugoslavia and even in the Soviet Union has spurred on the Chinese Communists in their relentless campaign for the continuation of the class struggle and against the revisionist heresy.

Interestingly enough, many Chinese not otherwise in sympathy with the government approve of its fight against the traditional class superiority of scholars. A woman of the former upper class told me of her astonishment when, during a business trip to Switzerland (before 1949), she saw the chauffeur of her Swiss business partner sit at the same table as his employer and eat the same food. In looking at present-day China, it should be borne in mind that only a small fraction of the people enjoyed the wonderful things the old China hands remember.

Nonetheless, the tendency of the new generation, or rather its elite, to become a new upper class more concerned with intellectual and material enjoyment than with ideological battles offers the only hope for a more liberal, more conciliatory spirit in China, even before it becomes a technological and economic world power.

6

The Terror of
"Communist Morality"

The hospital tour was over, and the director, the chief physician, a secretary, my interpreter, and I returned to the reception room, hung with the usual portraits of Mao Tse-tung, Liu Shao-chi, Chou En-lai, Chu Teh, Marx, Engels, Lenin, and Stalin. The 460-bed hospital, built in 1956, appeared neat and efficient, though somewhat old-fashioned by Western standards. Its achievements in bone surgery and skin grafting are very impressive so far as a layman can judge on the basis of photographs.

"Do you have any other questions?"

"Yes," I answered. "What is your main problem?"

The interpreter hesitated in translating the possibly embarrassing question, the director hesitated before replying, but then decided to:

"The chief problem is that our doctors are still very young and inexperienced. Their average age is thirty-one. So we older ones have to help them. No, this help isn't given in special courses, but primarily by the independent study of the writings of Chairman Mao Tse-tung."

"How, in your opinion, can reading Mao's writings help an inexperienced doctor?"

The ensuing lecture was delivered in all seriousness: The doctors learn from such reading how they can serve the people better, and they begin to understand why they must serve the people. They also learn that global developments follow certain laws, and they learn how the world—the subjective as well as the objective world—can be transformed. Above all, the study of Mao's works gives the young doctors the correct attitude toward historical and dialectical materialism, and because of this correct attitude they do better practical and scientific work. They all acquire a better understanding of the significance of their work within the framework of the struggle against imperialism and colonialism, and find in this the basic motivation for their activities. Therefore, they gladly and voluntarily study the writings of Chairman Mao Tse-tung.

Subtle Terror

The first time such a performance strikes a Westerner as ludicrous, but after the fiftieth repetition it ceases to be amusing. For the Chinese, who cannot board a plane after a two-month stay and take off, it is deadly serious. Whether the hospital director really had sacrificed his own mind on the altar of "socialist construction" or whether he had only fulfilled his "norm"—either is possible—makes no difference. The fact remains that the pressure of ideological terror has succeeded even in conversations on nonpolitical subjects, such as helping the sick, in replacing natural spontaneity with a kind of Party-made tape recording.

On the surface at least, this leveling of the mind is total, and the foreign visitor is constantly aware of the extent to which thought and speech have been reduced to mere Party rote. This, more than anything else, turns a stay in China, a country with so sublime a cultural past and great potential beauty, into a nightmare.

How is such uniformity achieved? Compared to Stalinist Russia or Nazi Germany, the terror in China is obviously less bloodthirsty and less brutal—except in Tibet. True, the Revolutionary Museum in Peking graphically tells the story, repeated proudly by the guide, of how the Communists killed more than 8 million Kuomintang soldiers during the Civil War. And it may be assumed that in the early years of the Communist take-over, almost as many people— owners of large estates and large or medium-sized farms, Buddhist or Christian priests—were murdered or condemned to a lingering death in concentration camps or prisons. But there were no wholesale purges of the Party apparatus à la Stalin. Every now and then someone is called for by the secret police in the middle of the night, but such occurrences are rare. The methods of intimidation are more subtle.

Everybody must belong to some official organization, from the Young Pioneers to the vocational and women's organizations to the Party itself. Of course, every organization is run and supervised by Party representatives. Factory workers usually live in housing developments belonging to the factory, doctors in the hospital, university students and professors, secondary- and frequently even primary-school pupils and their teachers in school dormitories or faculty houses. Leisure-time activities are organized by clubs attached to the factory or institution. Thus, at the workbench, in the canteen, in the library (while "voluntarily" reading Mao Tse-tung's works), in the theater group, and even in the housing block, everyone is constantly under the watchful eyes of a government representative who knows him, hears about everything he says, and knows when he is visited by an "outsider" or if he goes out often by himself, just as my interpreter always knew immediately if I returned late to my hotel after being entertained by journalists or diplomats of my acquaintance. There is no private life, no anonymity into which one can withdraw.

If anyone breaks ranks—perhaps devoting himself to a girl friend instead of to Party literature, or through an unseemly display of personal ambition instead of submissive acceptance of dull tasks or assignments to the steppes of Singkiang—he is not hauled away by the police. Instead, he is visited by "friends," activists fired by true faith, Party loyalty, and missionary zeal, whom he cannot escape: they work with him, live beside him, belong to the same club and the same vocational association, and attend the same indoctrination evenings. They will cling to him like leeches and not let go until he is convinced that his deviationist tendency, activity, or passivity is a vice, that his stubbornness has made him a social danger, that he serves the imperialists and enemies of the working class, and that it is his duty to support the cause of the people and therefore to abide by the wishes of the government. Confronted by such fanatics, who have behind them the full weight of the state machine and its propaganda apparatus, the individual does not have a chance. Moreover, in the cities he does not have the traditional support of the family clan, because he has been removed from the extended family. Solidarity of fellow workers against officialdom is almost non-existent. The heretic bows.

"Big Brother"

It has been said that China never knew any freedom, that it has always been governed by officialdom and by the traditions of the family clans. That is undoubtedly true, and there also can be no doubt that the slow erosion of the authority of the family through Western liberal ideas and the increasing corruption of officialdom created a vacuum which the Communist apparatus filled. But the authoritarian social order and rule rooted in Confucian tradition (and some non-Communist developing countries have similar social structures) gives people a modicum of freedom in the private sphere, if only in the "cellar" of life, a freedom which may be curtailed if a man advances to higher levels of active participation in public life. But most people do not yearn for public roles, at least not in countries that do not have a long tradition of democratic government in the modern Western sense. They live in their "cellars," happy to be left to their own small, private sphere, to their joys and sorrows, loves and hates, sense and follies, beliefs and superstitions. Occasionally the arbitrary acts of officialdom or the intolerant tyranny of a family head may strike like lightning, but without essentially or permanently endangering this private realm.

But under a totalitarian regime things are different. There the rulers want control over this "cellar." They demand belief and active acceptance. They are presumptuous enough to determine what is worthy of joy and sadness, of love and hate, what a man should learn, where he should live, and where he should work. One of my interpreters, married since 1960, has never lived with his wife and two children, because he and his wife are assigned to jobs in different cities and see each other only once a year.

Big Brother, present everywhere in China in the form of Mao pictures, watches everyone through his activist representatives. He is interested in everything: in the conversations of friends and whisperings of lovers, in fashions and dance styles and leisure-time activities. The total control of the souls and minds of all men is probably as utopian a goal as the classless society. But whereas in the Soviet Union and in Eastern Europe the demands of ideology are slowly giving way to demands for external displays of loyalty and the abjuration of active opposition, in China the attack of the righteous on the most secret recesses of man's soul is in full swing. And this is probably one of the major reasons for the conflict between Red China and the Soviet Union.

How successful are the Chinese Communists? In

walking through the swarming masses of people, children—my God, so many children!—and chickens in
the slumlike huts and backyards and alleys, it is hard
to believe that Big Brother can see everything, although, of course, the Party's eyes and ears are everywhere. And I also had the feeling that in the villages
I saw from my train window, the essential personal
life of the people cannot have changed too profoundly,
despite the people's communes, a feeling indirectly
confirmed by newspaper fulminations against peasants
who follow the tradition of slaughtering a pig and
spending all their savings for a wedding feast or
funeral.

The officials are always afraid that we foreigners
will criticize or ridicule their slums and "underdeveloped" villages and will use photographs and films as
arguments against Communist China; yet they are
proud of the ugly, dreary housing developments near
the factories and schools. But while abject poverty can
of course be a form of slavery (it is picturesque and
romantic only to a "master race" tourist) one cannot
help but feel that here the slums are perhaps the last
refuge, the "catacombs" of human spontaneity and
freedom. This is a frightening thought, because no one
can fail to hope that this martyred people be liberated
from misery, dirt, and backwardness. But if one sees
the "lucky ones," the teachers, physicians, employees,
and workers, whose lives are spent at their place of

work and who cannot escape their "commune" even during their free time through a hobby or retreat into the privacy of their family, then this progress seems a very dubious blessing. For here the penetration into the "free cellar" has become a lot easier and, so it seems to me, already has made great strides.

Since the food situation has improved, the all-penetrating propaganda has once more become highly aggressive. It permeates all phases of life and ever more loudly calls for the class struggle against all remnants of bourgeois mentality and all manifestations of revisionism. The Byzantine personality cult of Mao, the conquering hero, represents the acme of the propaganda assault. Mao's portrait looks down on every facet of life, and from his writings not only doctors, but also carpenters, masons, hairdressers, and kindergarten teachers are supposed to learn the correct attitude toward their professions and existence.

But continuous exhortations turn into noise, the hearing becomes dulled, and they lose their effect. The vital element in a totalitarian government is the existence of enough volunteer activists fired with the missionary zeal of true believers. That such people exist—as opposed to skilled technicians, managers, and workers—is evidence that the regime still possesses a strong ideological dynamism. The material rewards given these activists—special bonuses, promotions to better-paying jobs, preferential housing, etc.—fall far short of the privileges offered under Stalin. The desire to be on the side of virtue, or the fear of reproval and a bad conscience, is probably a greater psychological incentive.

Paragons of Virtue

The official interpreters isolate the foreigner as much as possible from contact with the activist system as from all the other realities of Chinese life. But the visitor who succeeds in eluding his chaperon can learn a quick lesson in how things work. For instance, a foreigner taking pictures on a street soon finds himself surrounded by a crowd of curious onlookers, among them usually one or two angry youths who threateningly hold a hand over the camera lens, prevent his retreat into the passive but obstructive crowd, and attempt to drag him to a police station or try to take his film away. Once while taking an evening stroll in Nanking, I turned into a side street that happened to lead to a building site. Not only was I taunted by the children as a Russian, but was accosted by an adolescent who wanted to know what business I had at the building site. It was no easy matter to dissuade him from carrying out his self-imposed mission of unmasking an imperialist agent and enemy of the people.

From the standpoint of the government, this is the ideal type of teen-ager, even if his excessive zeal toward a foreign journalist might prove embarrassing. They are the ones the foreign visitor to a school is introduced to with pride and who answer questions about what they want to become with phrases like: "It's unimportant to me how I serve the people. If the government wishes me to work in the people's commune, I'll do so just as gladly as if I were sent to the university."

The official model of the ideal Communist is Lei Feng, a soldier who died a few years ago and whose published diaries, genuine or not, overflow with high-minded phrases about serving the people. The precepts of helping one's fellow man, being kind to others, and showing consideration seem to correspond to our own code of ethics, but this similarity to universal ideals is deceptive, for these ethics are not intended as one person's code of behavior toward others. They are merely a device for disseminating the Communist morality, a social code under which everyone is meek and mild and righteously follows the leader. This is made obvious by the fact that underlying this guide to virtuous conduct is hatred, a merciless, fanatical hatred for everything bourgeois, capitalist, imperialist, and hence inimical to the working class.

Presumably the eyes of Big Brother cannot yet look into everyone's heart, and in the villages and back-yards and the slums, in which humanity and spon-taneity may still find a safe refuge, the system of

Lei Feng, the model of the new, virtuous Communist man.

activists is still not completely organized. And perhaps the rising generation is already developing the antidote of revisionism. But the China of today unquestionably bears a greater resemblance to Orwell's *Nineteen Eighty-Four* than any other country in the world.

7

In the Service of Propaganda

Everything must serve propaganda purposes. Not only newspapers, radio, and television, but also museums, archaeological excavations, theaters, movies, even Buddhist temples and the training school for the future cadres of the national minorities, such as the Tibetans, serve this end.

Stalin and Mao Defeated Japan

There are museums and ancient temples now turned into museums in which is displayed the art of more than two millennia of Chinese culture and which only tangentially serve political ends. The dispute with Moscow has added fuel to the fires of nationalism and stirred up pride in the country's long and brilliant cultural history. This is being exploited by the government in its domestic propaganda. Consequently, more and more ancient works of art, some of them of incomparable beauty, are being preserved, restored, and exhibited. Recent excavations have brought to light many sculptures, ceramics, and ornamental objects, supplementing the magnificent collections of ancient Chinese art in the museums of Taiyuan, Sian, and other cities—retreats from the sadness of everyday life.

But in the national historical museums, visited by foreigners as well as by organized groups of school children, factory workers, and soldiers, ideological categories prevail. Marxist social history governs the selection of exhibits. First came the primeval classless society, followed by the slave-owning, the feudal, and finally the bourgeois-capitalist order, which in turn was followed by the revolutionary change to socialism, the transition to the Communist paradise. Above vases, ornaments, or old documents hang socialist realist paintings of a peasants' revolt. The exhibits are a hopeless mixture of the historically genuine, tawdry contemporary imitations, and "educational" displays. Exquisite antiques furnish the background for a stereotyped travesty of social history. The mass of workers, peasants, and soldiers shunted through these halls must think that the history of China was just one continuous peasant uprising.

The display in the Museum of the Revolution offers a more contemporary falsification of history, including a misrepresentation of the part played by Mao Tse-tung in the first decade of the Chinese Communist Party. The guide, a young man who has been shepherding groups and individuals through these hallowed halls for the past five years, explained the pictures, documents, graphs, and models. He told of the Chinese struggle against Japanese aggression. Then he came to the summer of 1945. On August 8, the Soviet Union declared war on Japan and launched the Manchuria offensive. The Chinese Communist Army attacked the Japanese—and lo and behold, Japan capitulated. That the United States, unlike the Soviet Union, had been at war with Japan from 1941 to 1945 was never even mentioned. "If my memory does not deceive me," I interposed, "there was also Hiroshima." Discomfited, the guide admitted this, but, he said, "The American atom bomb killed only innocent people, not soldiers, and as Comrade Mao says, the outcome of a war is determined by the people, not by technical weapons."

In Moscow's Revolutionary Museum, Stalin is no longer mentioned. The Communists, those worshipers at the altar of History, are not too concerned with historical accuracy.

An Archetypal Village

In 1952, in the course of digging the foundation of a new house in Pan Po, near Sian, traces of a neolithic village were discovered. From 1954 to 1957, about one-fifth of the entire village, which is estimated to have had an area of 48,000 sq. yd., was excavated and roofed over, and the fascinating archaeological finds were put on display in a small nearby museum. All that remained of the prehistoric dwellings were the floors, marked with indentations for fireplaces, holes for supporting pillars, and traces of doorways. But with the help of these and other material clues, the archaeologists were able to reconstruct the huts and village, of which models were erected at the edge of the site. These reconstructed neolithic dwellings bear an uncanny resemblance to the houses in which the people of the region still live, 5,000 years later.

One might think that even though everything is tied to politics and ideology, archaeology would be exempted. Well, it isn't! On this site, we are told, can be seen the classless primeval society—the original people's commune, as it were—the paradise from which throughout history man was driven by the many exploiters, until the Communists began leaping toward the ultimate paradise on earth—the end of history, which resembles its beginnings. But if a sociological interpretation is absolutely necessary, then let it be said that the excavations themselves do not bear this out. The huts of different sizes, and the broad, deep ditch around the village, supposedly dug as a protection against wild beasts, is evidence of feuds with rival villages or clans. Some of the excavated graves held bodies buried with costly vessels, others with nothing. Some were lying face down, and one man, found in a kind of cellar, seemed not to have been properly buried at all, but simply had lain down to die, a starving prisoner. Ornamental pottery, baubles, and toys proved that the human quest for decoration and play, devoid of any social or utilitarian purpose, is as old as man himself. My Chinese companions were quite embarrassed when I pointed to these "counter-ideological" facts. The two ladies—the guide, an art history student from Shanghai, and the interpreter—took it with good grace; only the travel agency representative, who understood neither English nor anything else, became angry and disagreeable.

A Peking Opera

Peking opera and its counterparts in other cities of the country are a sort of Chinese musical, i.e., dramatic theater, with singers and dancers, accompanied by appropriately sentimental music. In the classical

plays, which employ mythological themes and pro-
tagonists like the sly and agile King of the Monkeys,
the masks, costumes, mime, and gestures are highly
stylized, especially in the Peking opera. But more and
more, modern plays are replacing the traditional theater. This is due not so much to popular taste or prefer-
ences, but to official decree. A monkey king, even
though he plays tricks on feudal lords, or a monk
with magic powers, even though he is evil and sepa-
rates lovers, has no place in the enlightened socialist
present, nor does love itself, unless it be love for the
Revolution, the people, Chairman Mao, or a tractor.

What is replacing China's highly developed traditional theater? Let us take a look at one of the sub-
stitutes, "Sparks Among the Rushes," a play produced
at the theater of the Peking Workers' Club. The setting
is a village during the Sino-Japanese War, after the
Nationalist Government and the Communists had
signed a truce in their common resistance against the
Japanese invaders. The village is briefly occupied in
turn by the Japanese, Kuomintang soldiers, and the
Communist Fourth Army. The local teahouse hostess
waits on all of them, but she is in fact a liaison agent
between the local and higher Communist leadership.
The villagers of course sympathize with the Communists, who are noble, helpful men of the people, and
in the face of the advancing Japanese, they hide four-
teen wounded Communist soldiers on a rush-covered

island in a nearby lake. The Japanese search for the
men in vain. The Kuomintang general, who occupies
the village next, collaborates with the Japanese commandant, a sly, slippery imperialist, with an evil,
malicious smile. The fat, brutal, stupid military chief
puts a close watch on the banks of the lake and its
island, where the heroic Communist wounded, on the
verge of starvation, only just manage to stave off
betrayal by a wealthy farmer. The comrades say that
bold action is called for, but the local political com-
missar, who rules with iron discipline, forbids any
action unless authorized by the higher Party authority. Thanks to the lady in the teahouse and a heroic
Communist youth, whose mother is captured and tor-
tured by Kuomintang soldiers because of him, the
necessary orders finally reach the island. In some
mysterious manner, the wounded are now able to
escape. At the wedding of the Kuomintang general
and the daughter of the Japanese commandant, the
Communist soldiers, miraculously recovered from
their wounds and privations, appear disguised as
musicians and peddlers, overcome the Kuomintang
and Japanese officers, liberate the village, and cele-
brate the happy ending.

The performance, a peculiar combination of propaganda and classical style and music, was highly professional. But the heroes and villains were blatantly
naïve caricatures, and no amount of acting talent

and skillful writing could make the play into a convincing human document.

"Satisfied or Not Satisfied?"

Broad caricature is even less persuasive on the screen, with its greater realism and audience identification. But in Mao's China, film makers have no choice. They must make crude propaganda pictures about saintly Communists and diabolical reactionaries, about the paradisical present and the hellish past, or the transition of a black sheep into a model of Communist virtue. The widely shown film "Satisfied or Not Satisfied?" is a fine example.

Time: the present. Place: a restaurant in Suchow, a picturesque tourist resort northwest of Shanghai. Main character: Waiter No. 5, an utterly impossible man. All the other waiters, and the customers, too, are blissfully happy, but he is surly, slams the plates on the table, brings the wrong dishes, barks at the guests, and snarls at them if they show displeasure. All his customers are dissatisfied, and they say so in the complaint book. His colleagues vainly try to make him see the right way. He regards waiting on others as beneath his dignity and refuses to recognize that serving the people is man's highest vocation. His sister, all sweetness and light, also tries to influence him. There is a glimmer of hope, but he remains stubborn, defiant, and self-willed, even after he has an accident

and all his dissatisfied, noble, self-sacrificing customers come to his aid, even after his co-workers give
him another lecture, citing the example of Lei Feng,
that epitome of Communist virtue.

Now comes a short flashback to the hellish conditions of "preliberation" China. Capitalist diners,
laughing sadistically, are taunting and beating up No.
5's father, also a waiter. They leave the restaurant
without paying their bill. This reminiscence of No. 5's
co-workers does make an impression on him. His resistance is further weakened when at a workers' party
a girl, one of his dissatisfied customers, sings a ballad
about Lei Feng compared to which the *Ave Maria*
sounds like rock 'n roll. Everybody listens with transformed faces. As if this were not enough, the girl
comes over to No. 5 and apologizes because in her an-
noyance she had been impolite to him in the restaurant and thus is guilty of an improper attitude. Later
he inadvertently puts on a jacket belonging to model
waiter No. 3, who had just been appointed a deputy.
Because he is wearing this jacket, No. 5 is whisked
away to address a group of workers on service to the
people. There he stands before the crowd, a black
sheep acting the role of a white one. He hesitates, stam-
mers, and finally plunges into a speech that ringingly
incorporates all the moral precepts he had been ex-
posed to during the previous weeks. His conversion is
complete: he becomes a model waiter.

Monks and Tibetans

In many places, including Suchow and Sian, the visitor can see Buddhist monks as well as Buddhist temples. But no amount of showmanship can prevent these monks from exuding monumental sadness. In response to my queries, I was invariably told that they and their temples were supported chiefly by donations from the faithful and remittances from overseas Chinese, and that they kept teahouses or tended small kitchen gardens. But if asked what effect the Communist government had on their lives and their religious activities, they say that they are supported by the state; also, that before the "liberation," Kuomintang soldiers used to stable their horses in the temple (because this is the standard story told in every temple one might conclude that it is part of the instructions for monks acting as guides and interpreters) but that now religion was free. On the walls—for example, in the Pa-Chin-San temple in Sian—there are pictures of the 1950 meeting of the Pan-Buddhist Union, a Party-controlled organization, in which priests and monks were made to toe the line.

Most Buddhist and Taoist temples and most Christian churches are closed. A few have been made into museums; only in a handful may religious services be conducted. They are shown to the visitors, but they are of little significance. There are no young priests

and monks to carry on. Some of the temples do have
valuable art treasures. It is impossible to tell whether
the monks who parrot the official line are crypto-
Communist stooges or whether they are forced to say
their piece and secretly hope that the visitor will see
through their feeble act and tell the world of their
unhappy lot.

The eradiction of religion—and that is the real
issue—is only one of the propaganda objectives. The
"coordination" of national minorities, particularly
the subjugated Tibetans, is another. In Peking, I visited
the Central Institute of Nationalities, founded in 1951,
where 2,500 students from Inner Mongolia, Sinkiang,
Kwangsi, Szechuan, Yunan, and above all Tibet were
being trained as the future cadres—that is, apparat-
chiks—of their peoples. These students are indoctrinated and they receive preferential treatment. They
are fully supported by the state, have large athletic
fields, and live only three or four to a room, instead
of eight or ten, as in other secondary schools and universities. Religion is respected, the guide assured me,
and as evidence he pointed to two small rooms, one
with a Mohammedan prayer rug and the other with
Tibetan religious objects. But he promptly added that
only the new students make use of these facilities, and
not many of them at that. As their education in dialectical materialism progresses, they shed their religious superstitions. The contempt with which the

guide, like all other government functionaries, spoke of religion was a pretty good indication of what a student from Tibet, for example, is subjected to if he should persist in his religious observances.

The adjoining hall contains exhibitions of the cultures of the national minorities, which the government supposedly fosters. In it, there is a display about the old Tibet: an enraged slave owner is seen in the act of chopping off the hands of a slave, while a cruel feudal landlord looks on. Next to this hangs a nauseatingly mawkish photo of liberated, beaming Tibetan peasants carrying a picture of Mao Tse-tung on their grain-filled cart: the grain, a sample of the harvest, is a present to the great leader. It is enough to turn one's stomach.

When I left the room, I met a group of armed women members of the people's militia.

8

Is There an Opposition?

Much of what goes on in China should be looked at as a kind of shadow play. If certain domestic practices come under heavy attack, it must be assumed that such things exist. If armed guards are seen in factories and even in schools, if soldiers are posted in every corridor of the Peking broadcasting studio building, there must be a reason. If a play at the Canton Opera is devoted to the theme of dissuading a young man from carrying out his plan for fleeing the Red paradise for the capitalist hell of Hong Kong, then such hankerings must be widespread enough to warrant an all-out attack.

In considering the question of the existence of an opposition, let us bear in mind that the survivors of the decimated, disempowered, dispossessed upper class of pre-Communist China are automatic enemies of the Communists. But the force and ideas of this natural opposition are based on an *ancien régime* that was defeated more than fifteen years ago and whose very bases of existence have been wiped out. It poses little threat to the government. Hence, fear of this defeated foe cannot be responsible for the Party's dogged and energetic prosecution of the class struggle. The shadow play raises the suspicion that there are more dangerous enemies within.

Apathy

A tangible feeling of passive, perhaps partly subconscious, discontent permeates the country. The Chinese in Southeast Asia, Hong Kong, and Taiwan are gay and colorful; across the border they are surly and cheerless. They neither smile nor laugh. The national coloration is a dull gray. Never before had I seen as gloomy a "people's festival" as the May Day celebration in Peking. The only spot where I found anything resembling spontaneity and gaiety was in an open-air performance of classical Peking opera scenes. The magnificent costumes imparted a sense of the glamour and glitter of days gone by. The brilliant fireworks staged by the government in its own honor every year on the first day of May and October cannot make up for the dullness of life under Communism, nor can the oceans of red flags brighten the depressing monotony of the dark-blue proletarian garb. Admittedly, Chinese women always dressed simply and wore dark colors —the North being traditionally more puritan than the more relaxed South. But the apathy is new. It is an achievement of the government, and it is this apathy which makes the streets of China seem so dreary and sad. Yet it will surprise no one who knows even a little about living conditions. Everyone is watched and feels watched; everyone is subjected to the joyless propaganda about the class struggle, about hatred against imperialists and revisionists, about vigilance and higher work quotas. Nor do the works of Mao Tse-tung make the liveliest and most entertaining reading. All hope for a better life through hard work or pure luck has vanished. Today, there is no such thing as a better life. Above all, the endless stream of exhortations, commands, and prohibitions has robbed life of the poetry of the old China, which permitted even the poorest coolie at least to dream of beauty and happiness.

A joyless May Day celebration.

Stalin still lives on in Peking. His portrait is carried in a May Day parade.

A Frank Conversation

General apathy, even conscious discontent with a sad, shackled existence, does not make an opposition, though it may lay the groundwork. It becomes a political factor only if it crystallizes into conscious criticism of the government.

In totalitarian countries, criticism is never voiced openly in the presence of casual acquaintances and certainly not before foreigners. At best, cautious hints are dropped. But there are highly revealing indirect symptoms, and if one is very lucky, even some revealing conversations.

As mentioned earlier, I once had the opportunity to talk privately with an English-speaking factory employee in southern China. (For obvious reasons the exact circumstances of this meeting must remain obscure.) A man in his mid-twenties, he had not participated in political life in the pre-Communist era. Both he and his wife came from the working class, so there was no question of any traces of a bourgeois past. Warming to the unhoped-for and unique opportunity of talking with a foreigner, he gradually opened up a little. He did not use official jargon: he said "Civil War" instead of "War of Liberation," and spoke of the "army which 'they' call the 'Liberation Army.' " His main criticism of the government was directed against the total control of all aspects of life, against the constant pressure of the subtle terror exerted by the propaganda machinery and the militant activists, and against the practice of giving top positions to incompetents simply because they had fought in the "Liberation Army." "Maybe as time goes by they'll learn something." Once he met a young Russian (when there still were some in China) who told him: "Stalin used to be a god, now he is a devil. How can we believe what they tell us?" And my Chinese acquaintance added that the sudden transformation of the erstwhile Russian friends into heretics was of the same order. In many things, he remarked, Khrushchev had been right—for example, about the atom bomb. He said that in the beginning the people's communes had been terrible—military camps, even concentration camps—but now things had improved.

Despite his rather slashing criticism, he also defended the government. After the "so-called liberation," many improvements were made—for the workers, at any rate. Therefore, he thought, and also because of propaganda, most people supported the government, particularly the women, who had had no rights at all. There was a good deal he did not like, but he felt that on the whole the good outweighed the bad, although he seemed none too sure. On the credit side, he unhesitatingly put down the abolition of prostitution and the general puritanism of government. This had been of considerable help in winning the women over to the Communists. He saw no alternatives to the present government, only the hope for gradual liberalization. As we took leave of each other, he repeatedly implored me not to tell anyone that he had talked to me, although he knew that I did not even know his name.

Apologists

Members of the Chinese middle class, whom the foreign visitor is more likely to come into contact with, do not dare such brash criticism. They try to defend the government, partly because they feel more vulnerable than a minor employee or a chance acquaintance, and partly no doubt because they try to see the positive aspects of a situation they cannot change, to find some meaning in a harsh fate. What are their arguments?

Communists, they say, have brought order to the country, and this in itself is an achievement. Before, everyone did just as he liked: almost every general mapped out his own, private political course; gangsters, frequently in collaboration with the police, ran Shanghai; soldiers were feared because they were undisciplined looters and thieves; those on the bottom of the social scale were at the mercy of every policeman, petty official, or anyone else more fortunate than they. Today they enjoy equal rights (or, to put it less kindly, the lowliest citizen has as few rights as anyone else), and the police and soldiers are disciplined. It is understandable, so they say, that strong, iron-fisted rule supplanted the inordinate individualism and hopeless disorder of the past. Surgery was called for, and it might bring about recovery, even though at first there is bound to be pain and suffering.

These people, who despite their reservations make far better advocates and propagandists for Communist China than all the phrase-mongering officials, are mouthing half-truths. There is something to what they say. The country was rotting and weak and divided, and its exploitation by the Western powers, Russia, and Japan cannot soon be forgotten. Peking, Nanking, and many small cities, even many villages, still have the walls needed not so very long ago as protection against a looting military, power-hungry generals, and roaming bands. Between the revolutions of 1911 and 1949, China never knew real peace. No country could live through so many years of war, civil strife, and foreign occupation without arriving at a point at which things could only get better—amid moans and groans, pain and sacrifice, yet with the glimmer of hope for a happier future.

The victory of Communism is thus understandable. But diagnosis of a disease does not in itself hold the promise of a cure. Nobody will deny that Germany in 1932–33 was sick and had every reason to seek surgical relief. The result of the surgery performed is now part of history. The question in China is whether Mao Tse-tung and his friends were and are good surgeons. Given the history of the past fifteen years, this seems more than doubtful, even if we were to ignore the suffering of the patient. The Great Leap brought famine, which in turn led to a disproportionate emphasis on agriculture, and as a result industry is stagnating. The inordinate demands made on the people have tired them out, and this let-up will have to be overcome by brutal whiplashing. Despite an annual population increase equal to the total population of New York City, vital economic resources are being allocated to the production of atom bombs (largely for propaganda and prestige purposes) and to the financing of world-wide subversive activities. And the economy itself is so directed and misplanned that more than half of the country's highly inadequate industrial capacity lies idle. Does this look like the work of competent physicians? Under these circumstances, does the cure justify the enormous sacrifices demanded by the surgeons?

But even the half-truths of the "critical apologists" deserve attention. The "on the one hand . . . on the other" type of criticism of individual problems is doubtlessly fairer than polemical criticism. But it hardly constitutes political opposition.

Class Struggle Against Whom?

As far as the Communist leaders are concerned, even limited, reasonable criticism is anathema, for they fear the very thing the critics want—an easing-up, the "liberalization" of the revolutionary fervor into what they call "revisionism." In talking with intelligent Communist officials, one can sense their concern. Being fanatical believers to whom ideology is more important than personal well-being, they are genuinely shocked by what has happened in Moscow (and worse still, in Belgrade)—i.e., the emergence of a new class which is becoming bourgeois, which puts standard of living and consumer goods above the ideological aims of world revolution, the classless society, and the establishment of true Communism, and which, under "revisionist" leadership, is engaged in pragmatic, opportunistic power politics. The fact that in more than four decades of power a Communist Party can so "degenerate" is a warning to the Chinese Communists. Stamp out the first symptoms of such a development, lest it happen here! Theirs is the historic task of proving that the road to Communism can be taken and adhered to.

Thus alerted by the "revisionism" of the Soviet Union and Eastern Europe, the Chinese Communists are all the more vigorous in combating similar manifestations in their own country. The failure of their

Great Leap, which via the people's communes was to speed the transition from socialism to the promised land of Communism, has made them painfully aware that the road to salvation is long and arduous, full of the dangers of revisionist seduction, and that it may take two or three generations to traverse. After all, they are still working with the man of the past, not the new, 100 per cent Communist man.

Vestiges of the man of the past are also to be found among the new generation, and they must constantly be suppressed by means of strict education. There is the tendency of high-school and particularly university students to regard themselves as an elite and to look down on the "proletarians." The young people who do not remember the time "before the liberation" are not frightened by the capitalist-bourgeois conditions of the past; on the contrary, those very conditions threaten to become the stuff of which their dreams of a better and sweeter life are made. One official even said that there exist "spontaneous capitalist forces," as, for example, the tendency of peasants to trade independently, which they do, thanks to their small private plots.

Thus, for a long time to come, the government will have to dwell side by side with the enemy: to build the economy, it must breed an elite and preserve an educational hierarchy; to feed the people, it must temporarily refrain from developing the people's communes beyond the present rudimentary stage and leave the peasants their private plots of land. And so the wicked, egotistical, bourgeois, capitalist mentality is constantly being nourished.

Once this train of thought is understood, the campaigns for intensifying the class struggle and the exhortation "Remember the past!" repeated in exhibitions, lectures, films, and plays, come as no surprise. Nor can there be any astonishment about a totalitarian system that admittedly has paralyzing effects on the economy but which, in the eyes of the true believer, who would rather starve than depart an inch from doctrine, is ideologically justified.

The Germ of Revisionism

An East European journalist recently told me that there is a people's commune in southwestern China in which the peasants were dividing up the collectivized land into private holdings. In Shanghai there is said to be a black market for Western jazz records. A singer of "decadent" songs from Cuba, the "socialist sister-state," was applauded so frantically by the young people—a cultural-political heresy—that his future scheduled appearances were canceled. In two or three of the higher schools I visited, it was admitted that there were isolated cases of students who had not yet found the "correct" attitude toward ideology.

In view of all this, can one speak of opposition to

the regime? Not really, if what is meant is a conscious political alternative, say, of the Chiang Kai-shek variety. At least a foreign visitor sees no evidence of it. However, from the government's point of view, opposition undoubtedly does exist. Revisionism is a clear and present danger; indications of its existence abound in the shadow play, in conversations, and other public manifestations. Moscow undoubtedly is aware of this. But even the revisionist Chinese are proud that Mao has dared to throw down the gauntlet before the little-loved "Soviet brothers," a pride born of nationalism, not of heroic ideological motives. The germ of revisionism was not brought to China by Western Communists. It came to life there spontaneously. It is nothing more nor less than human nature asserting itself. The same force that operated in the Neolithic village near Sian operates in present-day China—a striving toward individuality and spiritual latitude, the dream of a little joy and freedom and beauty.

At the moment, this passive opposition is of little significance. The true believers have an iron grip on the rudder; they see the threat and they are fighting it. Moreover, they are training cadres to succeed them. It may take a generation or two before a thaw sets in in China.

Art in a Blind Alley

China, it has been said, is not a country but a civilization, a culture, one of the oldest, greatest, and, at its
peak, one of the most refined civilizations the world
has ever known. How does this civilization fare under
the dictatorship of the proletariat?

In seeking an answer to this question, two basic
factors must be borne in mind: first, Chinese culture
has always been a highly aristocratic one, shaped by
the refined customs and tastes of a comparatively small
upper class, and far less deeply rooted in popular

tradition than, for example, the Japanese. Not until this century was any effort made to acquaint the people with their cultural heritage, and even then the emphasis was on literature rather than on fine arts and the theater. Second, Chinese art began to lose its vitality during the latter half of the Ching dynasty, largely in the latter half of the nineteenth century, long before the collapse of the *ancien régime* and certainly well before the Communist take-over. Artistic creativity, which had found its supreme expression in simplicity of form, lost much of its vigor, lapsing into stilted formalism and embellishment.

After this slow decline of its traditional culture, a renaissance, the creation of a new yet truly Chinese culture, would have posed a problem even without Communism. The Japanese are faced with a similar problem, even though their culture is more broadly based and the people more involved.

Art in the Service of Politics

Cultural development undoubtedly can be achieved by the Chinese, as the case of Ling Fong-ming, a painter living in Shanghai, attests. In his youth, shortly after World War I, Ling lived in Paris, where he came under the influence of modern Western painters, primarily Modigliani and Matisse. Although he shed some of the stilted traditions of Chinese painting, his art nevertheless remained thoroughly Chinese. Far from betraying his great heritage, he used it as a foundation. Although exhibits of Ling's paintings in Hong Kong have been highly successful, he does not enjoy official recognition in China. He is almost certain to rank among the century's most important Chinese painters, yet today he is merely tolerated by his government. The reason is simple: like every true artist, Ling Fong-ming serves art, whereas the government wants art to serve Communism, a demand more easily satisfied in theory than in practice. "Socialist" literature can be turned out and lay claim to being "literature" or "poetry," even though it may bear more of a resemblance to propaganda hackwork than to creative writing. In music, too, the problem is not too difficult. Chinese music, unlike Western music, has never played a significant independent role. It has found expression mainly in folk songs and in the theater (opera). Thus, in the case of music, one only has to change the plot; the same melodies that used to convey the emotion of individual love now sing of love of the Party. Similarly, the texts of folk songs can be changed. Under the heading "Traditional music—contemporary themes," a Chinese periodical recently published a list of folk songs retitled "Red Chorale," "Everyone is Praising the Commune's Vegetables," "Socialism is Good," and "Learn from Lei Feng" (the model Communist mentioned earlier). One can picture the fervor with which Tibetans sing "Ten Thou-

sand Years of Life to Chairman Mao Tse-tung," set
to the tune of an ancient Tibetan folk song. Record
shops feature such items as "The Long March Symphony," "Holy War Symphony," etc.

Classical Opera

When it comes to the theater, things are no longer
quite so simple. Plays set against the background of
the Sino-Japanese War or the Civil War or the present
do not pose any particular problem. I was told by
two officials of the Association of Theatrical Artists
in Peking that even in the classical theater there were
plays fraught with anti-feudalistic and anti-imperial-
istic significance. In times past, for example under
Mongol rule, the theater was an important medium of
intellectual opposition. (How mild compared to the
present-day rulers these oppressors who tolerated such
protests.) These plays, the officials said, could still be
staged today. Moreover, some old plays have been
rewritten just a little. Finally, there are new plays in
classical form and with historical settings written
along socialist guidelines, as for example one with the
theme "production without outside help" (in today's
context this means without Soviet technicians), which
takes place 2,000 years ago.

So far, so good, but the form of the classical theater
just is not socialist. It is operatic. Not only are entire
scenes and monologues sung, but the symbolism, the

nuances of expression in miming, tone of voice, gesture, and dancing, conveyed in an almost acrobatic manner, are at least as important as the story itself. This formalism for formalism's sake, this *l'art pour l'art*, does not please the new rulers. In their eyes, art is merely the superstructure built upon a sociological-economic foundation, and art dedicated solely to beauty and pointless enjoyment cannot be made into the superstructure of socialism and cannot become the expression of the new Communist man who wants nothing more than being a cog in the machine of a conformist society.

No doubt the ideologists would love to substitute pure propaganda plays for the traditional forms, but the people still want the latter. In the "culture palaces" of the larger cities, where for a modest fee the visitor is offered his choice of entertainment, the people bypass the dull propaganda shows in favor of classical opera and acrobats. Even—or perhaps mainly—the workers and their families are captivated by the fairy-tale magic of another, more beautiful and more glamorous world. Moreover, pride in the ancient culture, strengthened by the conflict with the Soviet Union, also has a part in the preservation of the deeply rooted classical opera.

To be sure, classical opera is gradually being overshadowed by modern propaganda plays. Still, it does survive and, as I had the opportunity to see at Peking's opera school, it is still being taught with all the refinements of pure, formal expression, acrobatics, make-up, and symbolic gestures. Of course, the students, who live at the school, are also being indoctrinated. The attempt to pour new, very red wine into old bottles has had some absurd repercussions. One incredibly crude propaganda film about the Civil War features singing in the style of the Peking Opera, but with formalism sacrificed to revolutionary romanticism. The result is an unbelievable hodge-podge of propaganda, sentimentality, and *Kitsch*.

Theater officials admit that they have not solved the problem. The old bottles contrast ludicrously with the new wine, but the authorities have not yet figured out how they can modernize without sacrificing tradition altogether. However, there is always the optimistic hope that the dedicated study of the works of Mao Tse-tung will eventually bring illumination. Should this happen, it would mean the slow but certain death of the great Chinese art of the theater.

The Academy of Fine Arts

The quandary is perhaps even greater in the medium of painting. In the place of "socialist realism," which is no longer quite acceptable because of its Russian origins, the government is promoting "revolutionary romanticism," which seems to mean pretty much the same thing as the doctrine of Zhdanov and his disciples. The term may describe the type of subject—Mao standing on a balcony at the founding of the People's Republic, a soldier of the Liberation Army striking a heroic pose, a beaming peasant atop his tractor—hardly the style of a painting. Neither the Ministry of Education, the Academy of Fine Arts, nor anyone else in the officialdom of art is able to explain what a revolutionary-romantic version of bamboo, a tree in bloom, or a landscape looks like. Moreover, since they do not reject the greatness of classical Chinese painting, but on the contrary would like to lay claim to it, they become enmeshed in hopeless contradictions. They thunder against formal art dedicated to beauty rather than the cause of a better world. When reminded of the perfection of a bamboo painting of the Ming period, they mumble something about the picture being good because of its positive influence and because bamboo is a symbol of heroism. Not a very Marxist answer!

Nowhere does the problem of reconciling tradition with the socialist approach loom larger than in the Peking Academy of Fine Arts. The dean of the department of oil-painting, Professor Ai Chung-chin, said that it is the function of art and the goal of the school to depict today's world and to be the superstructure of a socialist society. Today's world is one of agricultural and industrial development. A student who executes a technically good painting with the wrong subject or content has failed to understand the goal of the school. The dean admired an ancient painting in the reception room because its subject was corn.

My impression that utter confusion reigned was confirmed by a tour of the school. Some students were painting corn in the classical Chinese manner, while others were painting workers in the style of nineteenth-century European "realism." One student was allowed to paint a girl the way he wanted to because, he said, she was a tractor driver. One room was filled with priceless old Chinese paintings, another with paintings by teachers copied from photographs of late nineteenth-century European works, mainly Russian. In yet another room, students were trying to paint a photographic likeness of their model, an absolutely motionless girl wearing the uniform of the People's Army.

There is one ray of light in this dismal scene: if a student chooses an officially approved subject, he is comparatively free to paint as he likes, and undoubtedly some of the students have real talent. But they are not given any artistic and stylistic guidelines.

Chinese painting is taught in a special department, but it is nothing more than a sterile copying of the great art of the past, emasculated by the attempt to imbue it with a socialist and revolutionary-romantic spirit. And the imitation of Western art in its most unimaginative and hideous manifestation—Soviet

A "Socialist art" class.

socialist realism—has nothing to do with the distinctive character of Chinese culture. Ideological considerations bar the way out of this quandary. Asked for his opinion of the French impressionists, the instructor praised their technique but criticized them for portraying externals rather than real life and work. But in the past, Chinese painting did not deal with what he calls "real life" and "real work": it depicted man in a spirit of intellectual detachment for an unpolitical audience concerned with appearance or form.

Dictatorship of Taste of the Proletariat

The break with the great past and the beginnings of what promises to be a long march through a cultural wasteland are in evidence everywhere. Beauty is still accessible to the tourist, the art historian, and the remnants of the old civilized upper class. It is displayed in museums, preserved in a few temples, and faithfully restored in the Imperial Palace at Peking and the Ming tombs near Peking. But it is not alive. There are those who believe that within the family, the love of beauty is somehow being handed on from one generation to the next. Perhaps. But an understanding of Chinese culture, let alone its preservation, requires education and a refinement of taste. Present-day China offers no opportunity for cultural enrichment; sensitivity of taste cannot very well flourish amidst an atmosphere of brutal control of the arts.

In the art classes of the intermediate schools, the students paint stuffed birds or copy tractors from photographs. The one to two hours a week allotted to painting and music are spent in promoting art which "strikes a responsive chord in the masses," appeals to the proletariat, and educates the people in the tasks of socialist construction.

The Peking Factory of Handicraft Articles, founded in 1960, prides itself on having introduced industrial processes to replace the traditional skills formerly passed on from father to son. Now the workers read the works of Mao Tse-tung in order to become good craftsmen, but the results lead to the question of whether that is enough. In Soochow, an embroidery research institute supervises this former cottage craft and seeks to bring it into accord with the tastes of the masses. Upon the special request of Prime Minister Chou En-lai, two women were asked to embroider portraits of President Nasser from a photograph. The better one was to be presented as an official gift. Different embroidery techniques and subjects are expressions of Mao's "Hundred Flowers" theory. The manager of the institute held an embroidered copy of a classical Chinese picture to be an improvement over the original, because the colors were so much gayer. They were. Just like picture postcards, which are more cheerful than Sisley landscapes.

The decor of workers' model homes betrays the

prevailing taste: cheap color prints of a pink-cheeked Mao on the walls, crocheted antimacassars and *fin-de-siècle* furniture, enameled plates with mawkish likenesses of the sweet Lei Feng, machine-embroidered portraits of Lenin or Stalin, Mao or Liu. This sort of thing is also found in stores and handicraft shops. Only a few antique shops and museums offer something better. And even in the museums, next to pictures from the Ming or Soong period, one is likely to find a revolutionary-romantic scene showing the rebellion of proletarian peasants who in those days were not yet powerful enough to destroy the aristocratic Chinese culture but who now are.

10

The Isolated Middle Kingdom

Journalism in Communist countries bears only a superficial resemblance to what is generally understood as journalism. The foreign editor of *Ren Min Ri Bao* (*Peking People's Daily*), when asked about the function and purpose of his newspaper, was very frank: domestically, propaganda for government and Party policies among the masses; on the international level, to support oppressed peoples in their struggle against imperialism and revisionism. Not a word about gathering information or reporting news and facts.

117

Indeed, these exist only insofar as they provide material for propaganda, agitation, and polemics. For example, a strike in Belgium is cited as evidence of the aggravation of class antagonisms and of the general trend toward world revolution. Nothing is said about the reasons for and circumstances of the strike. Since the full truth is revealed in ideological dogma and the works of Mao Tse-tung, why worry about the facts of something that is happening in a far-away country? The foreign editor of the paper, which has a circulation of 1.65 million and is the most important in China, has never been to any other country except the Soviet Union.

Since Communist "journalists" are, in fact, minor Party or government officials in the field of propaganda and agitation, they have little understanding for the needs and demands of foreign journalists. The handful of regular foreign correspondents in Peking are cut off from all the facts they are supposed to report. This is as true of Russian and East European journalists as of Westerners. There are no press conferences, there is no freedom of movement, no contacts with residents. They are not even granted the right to visit the well-rehearsed schools and people's communes to which visiting journalists are taken. The only invitations extended to the regular foreign correspondents are to the pompous, dull official receptions for visiting foreign dignitaries.

An "Interview" With Foreign Minister Chen Yi

The traveling foreign correspondent is usually received by Foreign Minister and Vice Premier Marshal Chen Yi and granted what the Chinese choose to call an "interview." The questions asked must be submitted in advance in writing. Then, nothing more is heard for a while.

One day I was told that in an hour, Chen Yi would receive me. When the time came, it turned out to be a group interview, together with a Dutch and a Norwegian reporter, who had also submitted their questions in advance.

The interview consisted of Chen Yi's handing each of us a copy of his written replies to our questions, which had all been lumped together, and after delivering a short speech about China's economic development and its assistance to underdeveloped countries, he excused himself and left.

Here are some of the questions asked by me and the answers received:*

Q. The People's Republic of China is vigorously opposed to the "two-China theory"; however, it supports the attitude of the Soviet Union on "two Germanys." This is not well understood in my country. Please comment.

* Both the questions submitted and Chen Yi's replies were in English, and they appear here as originally phrased.

119

A. The two German states and the so-called "two Chinas" that you refer to are matters of an entirely different nature.

The objective fact of two German states is a result of World War II, whereas the so-called "two Chinas" is a plot hatched by U.S. imperialism. There is only one China, not two. China's Taiwan Province, occupied by Japan, was returned to China after the end of World War II. Where can the origin be found for the so-called "two Chinas"? What similarity is there with the two German states? In creating a situation of "two Chinas" or "one China and one Taiwan," the United States aims at detaching China's Taiwan Province from China, so as to perpetuate its occupation there. This is what the Chinese Government can never accept.

Q. Up to now the leadership of the Communist parties in most "white" and industrially advanced countries have, in the ideological dispute between the governments and the Central Committees of China and the U.S.S.R., tended to side with the Soviet Union. As this can hardly be a question of race and skin color, what do you consider the reason for this fact?

A. Our difference with the leaders of the Soviet Communist Party is a grave one, involving a whole series of major principles of Marxist-Leninist the-

ory. It is a difference between the Marxist-Leninist line and the revisionist line in the international Communist movement. You are quite right in saying that this is not a question of race and skin color. Revisionists are always a minority everywhere, including the "white" and industrially developed countries referred to by you. The broad masses of politically conscious and revolutionary people support Marxism-Leninism.

I had written down three more questions, linked with my second one, but unfortunately—and significantly—Chen Yi did not answer them. They were:

1. Do you expect the revolutionary line, as opposed to the revisionist, to be taken mainly by the so-called underdeveloped countries of Asia, Africa, and Latin America, and their Communist Parties? Or do you hold it probable that sooner or later the members of the CPs in the "white" countries will revolt against their revisionist leadership and force a change of policy?

2. If the answer on this last question is yes: Could this also occur in countries of Eastern Europe and particularly in Yugoslavia? And possibly even in the U.S.S.R.?

3. Do the government and the Central Committee of China consider the possibility of an initiative

to create a new Communist international organization?

My last question concerned Vietnam:

In the case of a military attack against the People's Republic of Vietnam, would China take military action to support the P.R.V.?

Chen Yi instead chose to answer a similar, but more vaguely worded question put by my Norwegian colleague:

Q. What would be the Chinese reaction if the war in Vietnam in one or another form should be extended to North Vietnam?

A. China and the Democratic Republic of Vietnam are both Socialist countries and fraternal neighbors, depending on each other like the lips and the teeth. In case of any encroachment on the Democratic Republic of Vietnam, the Chinese people will never stand idly by.

The answer was extremely cautious: teeth are mentioned only in relation to North Vietnam.

Class Struggle and War

The leaders of Communist China, if not the people, probably have a fairly clear idea of the power rela-

tionships, military, technical, and economic, involved in their confrontation with the United States and Russia. Despite all its threatening pronouncements, China is pursuing a foreign policy of extreme caution. When the Soviet leaders in the guise of peace-loving lambs accuse the Chinese of lusting for war, it is pure demagoguery. There is every reason to believe the Chinese protestations of their genuine desire to preserve the peace for many years, if not decades, because they need time to master their staggering economic problems and to build their new, classless society.

At the same time, the Chinese Communists dream of another kind of war, one that they would not have to wage directly but would merely foment, encourage, and assist. This is the revolutionary war, the "continuation of the class struggle by other means." Because they still believe in Marxism and its prophesies, they are convinced that in capitalist countries the rich get richer and the poor get poorer, thus intensifying class warfare, and that some day the proletariat, under the leadership of the Communist Party, must and will take up arms against its "oppressors." Just as they themselves began and ultimately won a civil war against the "Chiang Kai-shek clique," so the poor, oppressed workers in, say, America will some day launch and win the battle against the "Wall Street clique," and it will be the duty of the socialist countries to encourage and assist them in their struggle.

These notions, constantly drummed into the people by the propaganda machine, can flourish only in total ignorance of the outside world. Even today, China still calls itself Chung Kuo—the Middle Kingdom. The age-old feeling of cultural superiority of the Chinese upper class, which thought the "barbarians" of neighboring countries utterly unworthy of notice, has entered into a fatal partnership with the dogmatic smugness of the Marxists, who, familiar with the "laws" governing world history, feel that they need not bother to understand specifics.

The isolation, i.e., the self-isolation, of China is unbelievable—and frightening. Neither newspapers, films, television, radio, nor any other medium tell the people, high and low alike, anything about what is happening in the world outside. No foreign films are shown. Newsreels show the arrival and reception of delegations from Africa, Asia, or Latin America, of awards being given to shock workers or elite army units, etc. Except for an occasional nineteenth-century work, no foreign books are to be found in the bookshops; there are no foreign papers, not from the Soviet Union nor from Eastern Europe. There are no longer any foreigners in China, except for the handful of diplomats in Peking and the visiting "delegations." Even in a former international center like Shanghai, foreigners are stared at like some exotic animal in a zoo. Crowds gather to watch a foreigner leaving a theater,

a movie house, or a shop. Peking is the only place where people do not gape at foreigners like at some glamorous movie star. Because the crowds are frankly curious, not hostile, there is something rather touching about this. An African visitor, however, who had aroused the usual interest stirred up by a foreigner, mistakenly attributed this to his color. Enraged, he climbed on a shop counter, glared at the crowd, and shouted in English: "Go ahead! Look at me—the ape from the jungle!" This happened in Shanghai, where not too long ago ships from all over the world docked daily and where people of all colors were part of everyday life. The government has launched a campaign under the slogan "Do not stare at foreigners." But on the basis of personal experience I can state that the results are nil.

State Visits

The visits of foreign heads of state, official delegations, and representatives of foreign Communist organizations are a triumph of Chinese stage management, a sharp contrast to the attitude toward "ordinary" foreigners.

The show begins at the Peking airport, where military units stand in parade formation, brass bands blare, and hundreds of pennant-waving girls in festive attire smile. Well-rehearsed demonstrations of enthusiasm erupt when the foreign guest is greeted by

125

President Liu Shao-chi, Prime Minister Chou En-lai, and other high officials. The route to the center of the city is lined with more pennant-waving, colorfully clad, joyously enthusiastic young people, who had assembled in strict military formation one or two hours earlier. The usually dull, joyless, colorless, grim Chinese scene suddenly comes alive with color, freshness, joy, even glamour. Lipstick, a decadent, bourgeois cosmetic normally not to be seen in China, now is on the lips of thousands of schoolgirls. A portrait of the distinguished guest, ten times as large as life, is conspicuously displayed at a strategic location. Comes evening, well over a thousand guests gather for a banquet in the Great Hall of the People; two orchestras play, a magnificent ten-course dinner is served, speeches are made, national anthems played, and toasts drunk. These receptions always follow the same precise ritual, but the guest of the day does not know this; deeply flattered, he sees only the honor bestowed on him.

The majestic pageantry that characterizes state and delegation visits is aimed not only at impressing foreigners with the grandeur of Communist China, but also at suggesting to the Chinese people that the entire world except a few wicked imperialists and revisionists, but principally the nonaligned, third world of the developing nations, is fraternally bound to China. Clearly, world revolution is on the march, and while

Chou En-lai escorting a delegation from Tanganyika at an official banquet in the Great Hall of the People in Peking.

it may be a long march, ultimate victory is certain. Moreover, in the Communist world of tomorow, or the day after tomorrow, in view of the betrayal by the Soviet revisionists, Peking will become the Red Mecca, the focal point.

This Communist Chinese chauvinism is not without its dangers. China's total isolation from the rest of the world, known to the people only through the gross distortions of propaganda, makes for a serious over-estimation of its power and the loss of all realistic sense of proportion. The self-righteous conviction that China has a lien on salvation would seem to justify the kind of ideological, political imperialism that in principle knows neither bounds nor boundaries. In contradistinction to this, China's foreign policy is realistic, restrained, careful, and aware of its limited possibilities. But the question arises whether today's—and above all tomorrow's—Chinese Communist leaders will not become prisoners of their own propaganda, and whether they can continue to maintain a balance that contradicts their ideological lack of restraint. The question becomes even more acute if the "world revolution under the overlordship of the Middle Kingdom" should fail to fulfill its expectations.

11

From Peking to Moscow

The conflict between Peking and Moscow is almost
tangible. When seen at close range as a contrast of
atmosphere, outlook, behavior, living standard, architecture, theater, fashion, etc., then one cannot possibly
continue to believe that all that is involved is a power
struggle between ambitious Communist leaders.

"On Our Own"

Everywhere in China there are signs of the conflict.
In all hotel corridors, in hotel restaurants, at airports,

in railroad stations, etc., anti-Soviet propaganda material is distributed in Chinese, Russian, English, French, German, Spanish, Vietnamese, and Arabic—pamphlets with titles like *Origin and Development of the Differences Between the Leadership of the CPSU and Us*, *The Leaders of the CPSU Are the Greatest Splitters of Our Time*, *Defenders of Neocolonialism*, *The Truth About the Alliance Between the CPSU and India Against China*, and so on. On the train between Canton and Peking, the sleeping-car porter even brought such pamphlets into the compartment. Everywhere there is the slogan "On Our Own," an appeal to national ambition, urging the people to carry on their economic and technological development without foreign aid, without the Soviet technicians who deserted China in 1960. This withdrawal, coming in the very year when the Great Leap Forward and the people's communes, in conjunction with unfavorable weather conditions, plunged the country into a great crisis, undoubtedly hurt China badly and generated genuine bitterness. The courage with which the government faced up to the challenge and refused to be disheartened probably did more to gain it popularity than anything else it had done during the past ten years.

The defiant "On Our Own" attitude sometimes results in things like the re-invention of simple machines known for many years in advanced countries, and their manufacture with inadequate labor and low-

Monument to the impermanence of earthly things: the palace of Chinese-Soviet Friendship in Shanghai.

grade materials. While the technical results are not always impressive and the waste of energy, materials, and time is frequently considerable, the unconquerable will to achieve self-sufficiency is admirable and should not be underrated. Less admirable, if true, is the practice reported by the Russians, whereby trade-marks on Russian-built machinery are filed off and Chinese names substituted.

Soviet "Glamour"

The Aeroflot Tupolev of the Peking-Moscow run I boarded (via Irkutsk and Omsk) had two hostesses. One was a massive blonde Valkyrie; the other might have come straight from Air France—tall, slim, beautiful, with a smart hair-do, faultless make-up, and red nail polish. On the whole, Khrushchev's exhortation to Soviet women to be more elegant than their Western counterparts has not as yet had conspicuous results, but coming from China I was astonished by the comparatively large number of well-dressed Moscow women with the latest (or next-to-latest) hair styles and make-up. In Moscow shopwindows I saw pictures of models wearing jewelry, as glamorous and smiling as brilliantly as those in Western fashion magazines. And in the evening, the young people of Moscow's elite can be seen dancing, if not the Twist or the Frug, perhaps the Cha-cha-cha, something that would be unthinkable in China. To a visitor coming from the West, all of this may seem shoddy, and the prices for halfway attractive, well-made goods are still exorbitant measured by Soviet wages. But to the visitor coming from a two-month stay in China, the trucks, private cars, and taxis, the shopwindows, the occasional modern Western-style buildings, and all the other earmarks of city life make Moscow look like Paris.

Are the Chinese right? Has the Soviet Union become bourgeois, deproletarianized, revisionist?

The Village Landlord as Martyr

At the Vakhtangova Theater in Moscow, a visiting troupe from Leningrad performed "Dyelo," by A. V. Suchovo-Kobilin. The play is set in the middle of the nineteenth century, and the main character is an elderly man who owns three villages. Aha, very obvious! The rich landlord as villain, and of course an exploited serf or tenant as hero. That is exactly how it would be in China. But not here. The bureaucrats are the villains. They have discovered a minor irregularity in the old man's personal file (*dyelo* in Russian means *file*), and use this discovery to blackmail him. They ruin his daughter's reputation, then force him to sell two of his villages so that he can pay the price of their silence, and hound him to death. The minor bureaucrat who authored the scheme is cheated out of his profits by his superior, but, so he tells the audience, he is going to dig up another file, find another victim, and get the money he was cheated out of. The villainy of the bureaucrat is emphasized by the ending, in which, etched against a dark sky, he climbs up a stairway into an almost unreal twilight while vowing that "we bureaucrats" will always come out on top, over the heads of all men and all peoples.

The visitor just arrived from Peking is incredulous. Can this be true? The owner of three villages, an honest man victimized by injustice, is portrayed with stirring compassion. And the state official—the fact that he is a Czarist bureaucrat is reduced to insignificance in the final scene—is evil personified. The moral confrontation is not between the selfish individual and the heroic masses, but between an oppressed individual and the diabolical state machinery. And class consciousness, the essence of Marxism, is so irrelevant to the plot that a typical representative of the feudal upper classes is depicted merely as a suffering human being, with none of the familiar trappings of caricature.

Perhaps the Chinese are not altogether wrong in thinking that the Soviet Union has strayed from the path of Marxism.

"Economic Miracle" Communism

The most striking difference between Moscow and Peking is in the opportunities for personal contacts.

At the Irkutsk airport, barely ten minutes after touching Soviet soil, I was engaged in a completely normal, relaxed conversation with a local girl, a student of French who was getting practical training as an Intourist employee at the airport. Admittedly, we did not discuss any vital political issues, but in my two months in China, I had had exactly one similar exchange. In Moscow that evening I had an equally friendly conversation in the restaurant of my hotel with a young engineer who sat down at my table after inquiring politely whether the seat was vacant. In response to my questions, the Intourist interpreter described herself as a Communist and atheist, and showed displeasure at the mention of Stalin, Stalinist architecture, high prices, etc. But in China, were she to behave with like nonchalance, she would risk the charge of having become "bourgeois." No foreigner would ever dare visit a Chinese in his home for fear of endangering his host's safety or, at the very least, causing him difficulties. In Moscow it is possible to do so, if perhaps not too often.

In all conversations with high or low Soviet officials, it is made surprisingly clear that compared to China, ideology plays only a minor role. Russia is chiefly preoccupied with economics, technology, production figures, and living standard. This is illustrated in the Revolutionary Museum, which traces the history of the CPSU from pre-Revolutionary times up to the present.

135

For the entire period from Lenin's death (1924) until today (except for the "Great Patriotic War"), there is practically no politically significant display. The emphasis is on economics, Five-Year Plans, industrialization, electrification, mechanization of agriculture, etc. Stalin is not mentioned.

However, Moscow shares Peking's conviction that Communism will ultimately triumph over capitalism. But the Chinese believe that this victory must and can come about through the combination of ideological dynamics and the active prosecution of the world revolution; the Soviets base their hopes on the Communist economic miracle. The Soviet economy—so their argument runs—has in the last few decades expanded more rapidly than the American economy, and therefore it will one day overtake it. When this happens, people all over the world will naturally choose the social system that offers them the greatest material rewards. The Russians have absolutely no doubts on that score. They appear to be even more concerned about the standard of living than the Americans, and seem to have come to regard Communism as little more than a production method in the service of a self-confident great power. The Chinese, on the other hand, consider Communism as the definitive solution to all the ills plaguing society, a socio-philosophical doctrine that will bring happiness to all mankind. Understandably, they are disturbed by any hint of revisionist tendencies. Of course, it can be said that the Chinese Communists themselves are not exactly spotless in practice: the income of their elite is at least ten times that of the average worker. But that, of course, is another matter.

Seen from Peking

There is a saying that *"Chacun est le bolchéviste de quelqu'un."* Today it might be said that *"Chacun est le capitaliste de quelqu'un."* In Western eyes, the Soviet Union is a Communist country, a one-party dictatorship determined to bury free, democratic societies, and strong enough to constitute a menace to the West for years to come. It is highly doubtful whether Russia's "de-ideologization" or "liberalization" would change things much, even if it were even greater than it is today.

Seen from Peking, however, the picture is quite different. In the Great Hall of the People, I found myself sitting next to correspondents of *Pravda, Izvestia, Tass,* and Polish and East German newspapermen. Surrounded by politically aggressive but polite Chinese, it was a strange experience to find oneself almost in the same camp with these "revisionists," swapping political jokes with them. (The Yugoslavs, of course, are in a class by themselves; they are practically indistinguishable from West Europeans.) Race has nothing to do with this alignment. The cleavage has occurred because the Chinese Communists are dedicated to the eventual establishment of a Communist society along dogmatic lines, whereas the Russians have begun to think in terms of missiles and butter, of high-heeled shoes and *la dolce vita*. Despite the West's sharp disagreement with the Russians, there exists an area of agreement. But the utopians of the Middle Kingdom, who believe in the power of their ideas and are prepared to fight for them and for their own pride at the cost of tightening the people's belts, and to some extent their own, are frightening. Yet they are somehow more impressive.

12

China and the World of Tomorrow

In the 1930's, when Japan became aggressive and expansionist, the West spoke of the "yellow peril," meaning the "yellow" race, the nations of fierce, slit-eyed, sinister, strange people. Will China become the "yellow peril" of tomorrow, or are we threatened by a "red peril," a fanatically aggressive ideology, which, seeking international, world-wide influence, wishes to incite the "underdeveloped have-nots" of South Asia, Africa, and Latin America against all the

A typical commune—many agricultural chores are still performed manually.

Village scene near Canton.

political, cultural, social, and economic institutions of
the developed north?

At the moment, the two are almost inseparable.
Ideological fervor and the nationalistic pride of a
great country emerging from a century of weakness
and racial humiliation are interrelated. Today and
in the immediate future, China's power is and will
remain limited, but its revolutionary ideology might
find fertile soil in countries whose elites are determined at all costs to lift themselves out of poverty and
backwardness into "modernity" and who are not yet
immune to the virus of the Communist utopia.

The "Yellow Peril"

At the acme of China's long history, the power of
the empire extended far beyond the borders of Red
China. Outer Mongolia, Korea, Siam (Thailand),
Nepal, much of Indochina, and parts of Burma had to
pay tribute to the "Son of Heaven" in Peking. Since
China has remained much stronger than these relatively small, lowly neighbors, it may be assumed that
today's rulers see themselves as the heirs of the old
dynasties and that they dream of once more making
these countries into what used to be known as "vassal
states," and which in Communist terminology are
called "friendly people's republics," i.e., satellites.
The Chinese have succeeded in the cases of North
Korea and North Vietnam, but all further attempts at

direct or indirect expansion have come up against American military power or, in the case of Outer Mongolia, which is part of Soviet Russia's satellite empire, the power of the U.S.S.R. What, then, are we to make of Red China's military strength, particularly with regard to Vietnam?

In sheer size, the Chinese armed forces are the strongest in the world, with approximately 2.7 million men and a potential of three to four times that number in case of war. Most of this manpower is in the land army. China's fleet is made up of some Soviet U-boats and a number of fast torpedo boats. Its air force, according to Japanese sources, is equipped with around 2,600 planes, of which only about 100 MIG-19's are modern craft. Moreover, there is a shortage of replacement parts and jet fuel; consequently, pilot training has been curtailed.

Despite differences of opinion in the highest reaches of the country's political and military leadership, the Chinese land army is still largely a nonprofessional body. Soldiers are assigned to harvesting, road-building, construction of dams and canals. By modern standards, they are inadequately equipped. The Soviet Union stopped its arms shipments in 1960, but China has since increased the domestic production of artillery and light weapons and has improved troop equipment. A quarter of the army training program is devoted to political indoctrination, another 15 per cent to instruction in reading, writing, and arithmetic. For the most part, the soldiers are simple peasant youths with little technical skill. Western and Japanese experts believe that the level of training of the lower ranks has fallen off since the Korean War, when the "People's Liberation Army," a product of the Civil War, still had extensive battle experience. In considering China's readiness for waging a war of aggression, it must also be borne in mind that, on the whole, rail transport and roads are poor, especially in southern China. The country would be virtually helpless in case of attack by a superior enemy air force, and rapid movement of large bodies of troops wellnigh impossible.

But China also has its strong points. Its tough and tenacious soldiers are relatively well off, and this, combined with their intensive political indoctrination —hatred of the enemy who, they are told, is a criminal or the hireling of criminals, and dedication to the cause of "liberated" China—makes for a high degree of moral stamina, willingness to fight, and fanaticism. Their enthusiasm possibly might infect the people with whom they come into contact. The tradition of guerrilla warfare—rapid movement, surprise attack, and encirclement when the enemy is weak, evasion and disguise where the enemy is strong —is still alive and being nurtured by officers under the influence of the old Civil War veterans at the top.

Such tactics are virtually useless in open terrain, as for example in Mongolia, but they can be dangerous in the jungles of Southeast Asia, above all if, through the traditional and proven combination of propaganda and intimidation, they are able to win over the local population and be kept informed of the movement and plans of the enemy without much risk of themselves being betrayed when they have to retreat and hide.

But in guerrilla warfare, large armies cannot be deployed, except perhaps in China itself and in some areas of Indochina. What is needed is a small number of specialists. On the other hand, except for a few elite divisions, China's huge army and strategy are not geared to mass deployment. The army is too vulnerable to attacks by a superior air force and, possibly, tactical atomic weapons. Thus only two forms of offense seem likely: (1) the support of local—i.e., native—guerrilla forces by small, specialized units, or (2) the attack of selected elite divisions on weak countries that do not have strong American support, such as the Himalayan campaign against India— that is to say, a campaign with a limited military objective. In both these instances, the mass of well-indoctrinated but poorly equipped and trained soldiers is superfluous and worthless. This would seem to indicate that China's leaders, in resisting the military's pressure to make the People's Liberation Army into a modern professional army and by clinging to the idea of a mass army, are thinking in terms of defense, not offense. But defense against whom? Possibly against an invasion of American-supported Nationalist troops from Taiwan and against local uprisings. Whether or not their fear is well founded and realistic is immaterial. The fact remains that it does exist and can be explained partly by the fact that the Communist leaders know as little as we do about what the Chinese people think and feel in the secret recesses of their minds and hearts, and partly because the American mind and American policy are as alien and incomprehensible to the Chinese as the Chinese mind is to Americans.

But in trying to estimate the "yellow peril" of military offense, one simple factor is of signal importance: by launching a large-scale military offensive, Peking risks a war with the United States, and in view of the Sino-Soviet conflict, China cannot rely on the Soviet Union's readiness to run any risks for its "yellow" comrades. (This, incidentally, was stated quite openly by Chou En-lai in an interview in the Cairo weekly *Al Mussawar* of June 3, 1965). War with the United States would mean risking the destruction of China's cities and industry, including its atomic plants. China would not be able to retaliate, because it does not yet possess sufficient nuclear strength and, more important, missile delivery power. Moreover, the Chinese, their propaganda to the contrary, know only too well that the American (and Soviet) nuclear power is not a paper tiger. No country in the world will openly tell a political enemy that under no circumstances will it go to war. That would be an open invitation to political blackmail. But all indications, all unofficial Chinese pronouncements, and all power-political considerations point to the fact that Red China at this stage of events would wage a major war only if pushed to the wall.

The "Red Peril"

Up to April 17, 1956, the date on which the Cominform was dissolved, the Soviet leadership was in possession of an official instrument for controlling and directing the world-wide Communist movement and the numerous international and national front organizations of youth, students, women, farmers, journalists, and so forth. After that day, under Khrushchev's policy of peaceful coexistence and the toleration of the "individual national road to socialism," Moscow's international ties became a bit looser, though they still existed. Moscow remained the center of international Communist activities, laying down the line to the world movement, except for Yugoslavia, China, and Albania. Today, Peking has become a center of world Communism, vying with Moscow for influence and leadership from New Zealand to Brazil to Romania. National Communist parties have split into pro-Soviet and pro-Chinese factions, as have international Communist organizations. The Chinese are in the process of setting up a Peking-controlled and -directed Communist International, along the lines of Stalin's Comintern of the 1920's and early 1930's and its successor, the Cominform. The impact of this movement, which as yet has no official name or shape, cannot be judged at this stage.

That the revolutionary impulses emanating from Moscow have lost much of their potency in the past ten years is beyond discussion. The industrial "proletariat" of the Western countries has become so bourgeois that there is little hope for revolution. In the neutralist countries—e.g., India, Egypt, and Algeria— Moscow, in an effort to keep these countries out of the Western camp, relied on and entered into alliances with non-Communist and anti-Communist national leaders and basely deserted the true revolutionary forces, just as Stalin deserted Mao Tse-tung for Chiang Kai-shek because Mao's chances of carrying out a successful revolution seemed very slim.

But suddenly, Peking appears on the scene, summoning the revolutionaries throughout the world to its banner. Mao's fighting doctrine, aimed at the agricultural proletariat, propagates guerrilla warfare of the technically weak minority in uncharted territories and holds up its own success as a shining example. Undoubtedly it has great appeal for the downtrodden masses and the ambitious, half-educated students and "intellectuals" of the developing countries beset by overwhelming social problems.

China has another advantage over the Soviet Union: it is a "colored," underdeveloped nation. The stronger the feelings of inferiority of the colored nations, the greater the resentments of the underdeveloped countries, the more imposing is the challenge posed by a backward, "yellow" China that possesses the atom bomb. True, on the basis of long experience, Southeast Asia fears Chinese imperialism and also knows that Japan, also a "colored" country, has achieved a much higher level of development. But who in Africa or Latin America knows that as long as two thousand years ago, the Chinese no longer were a primitive tribe?

We in the West, having lost our belief in ideology —or perhaps never having had one—tend to underestimate its appeal. We believe in the supremacy of material and technical achievements. If we speak of a Chinese danger in the Sudan or in Venezuela, we mean the presence of Chinese soldiers. But that is not the danger. The real danger are the people who have had a smattering of education, who have read—and half-understood—a few books, who feel entitled to high-level positions which they do not get, and who, seeking personal power, want to overthrow the existing regimes. They seek ideological motivation and find it in half-grasped Marxist theory. They see themselves in the role of a Mao or Fidel Castro. They are invited to Peking, where they are received with undreamed-of pomp; they are influenced, trained, indoctrinated, and encouraged in the very seductive belief that a determined minority using the right tactics can eventually wrest power from the majority. They return home, and through the force of their commitment they are able to gain the support of another 4–5 per cent of the population—the dissatisfied, miserable, resentful of this world. A few Chinese experts help them with advice, money, and arms to build a partisan fighting force, and they become involved in a romantic, adventurous undertaking which represents their only hope to become popular heroes and to capture the much-coveted seats of power. And then it all starts: bombings, political assassination, demonstrations, newspaper headlines, vociferous propaganda, the admiration of naïve followers, the fear, the self-importance. Then comes another invitation to Peking and with it the growing belief in one's own destiny, of being the benefactor of the people carrying out the laws of history. Through a combination of unbridled propaganda and intimidation, of lying promises and terror, such an active minority can force its will upon a majority that does not know what it wants, even though those who believe in majority rule may find it difficult to understand this. The Chinese Communists have much theoretical and practical experience in this sort of thing, which Marxist theory preaches very openly—i.e., the dictatorship of the proletariat. A revolutionary minority in Africa, Latin America, or South Asia which gains the support of such a successful power, be it in the form of advisers, money, or arms, or in the form of two-year leadership training in guerrilla and psychological warfare, can become quite effective.

If we accept Mao's tenet about the fish and the water in which the fish either survive or die, then the water temperature in large areas of the world is not unfavorable to the revolutionary Communist fish. But a rebel band that hopes to become a revolutionary civil war force must have ideological guidance and disciplined organization. When the once unlimited supply of dynamic ferments from Moscow became irregular, Peking took over. The continued supply of these world-wide revolutionary impulses and their organizational props are assured for some time to come. And the rulers of present-day China have proved that they are ready to divert some of their limited financial resources to the cause of world revolution and to the development of the disproportionately expensive atom bomb, regardless of the cost to their own people.

Glimmer of Hope for the Future

The leadership of Red China is composed of revolutionaries with a background of civil war, propaganda, guerrilla warfare, ideology, and organization of political power in their own country. They know very little of the rest of the world; they have no inkling of modern technology and sociology. These things are of little interest to them. Their knowledge and their view of the world are limited to Marxist theory as interpreted by Mao Tse-tung.

But China now has the atom bomb and has had its first encounters with modern technology, science, and industry, with problems of diplomacy in the contemporary world, with foreign trade and currencies, with management and trade balances, with elites and cost accounting. This vast nation demands its right to life, and the regime will have to meet this demand with something more than propaganda if it wants to survive. A new generation, which did not participate in the Long March, is coming to the fore, and it is concerned with accomplishment and success rather than revolutionary slogans which, after more than fifteen years, have lost their appeal.

We know from Russia that the technicians and managers can coexist with the ideologists and revolutionaries and that the most blatant class differences do not necessarily prevent a country from assuming the public stance of the "classless society." But Russia has also taught us that a country loses its reputation of advocate of the poor and underdeveloped when it becomes an arrogant, aggressive, imperialist great power. Today, the Chinese army is still a "proletarian people's army," and as long as its atom bomb remains a prestige weapon rather than a usable military one, it does not have to accommodate itself to the laws of modern warfare. But once technology becomes paramount, then it will perforce bring about structural reform and modernization of the army and military thinking, and when that happens, a chasm will open up between the reality of a modernized army and the concept of guerrilla civil war. This was made unforgettably obvious in 1956, when Soviet tanks rolled against the Hungarian workers.

I believe it will take many years before China becomes a modern industrial state with the economic and technical foundation of a major modern military power. And during this period, the Chinese Revolution will recede into the dim past; China's future elite will take its position in the world for granted. It will not share the present leaders' aggressiveness born of resentment over the humiliation of China. This future elite, like the leaders of the Soviet Union today, will wield greater power than Mao and his coterie, and therefore it will be forced to learn that power brings with it responsibility and that it is limited by the power of others. Even today, China already stands to lose a lot which it has built up at such great cost. Once it is in a position to wage war against a modern power like the United States or the Soviet Union, it will stand to lose as much as the Soviet Union, and it will therefore have to invent something like "peaceful coexistence." And the have-nots of Africa will find out to their dismay that the Chinese will hold their own shirts of fairly decent quality dearer than the ideological wraps of the revolutionary Africans.